Lonely planet

POCKET

ROME

TOP EXPERIENCES • LOCAL LIFE

PAULA HARDY, ABIGAIL BLASI

Contents

Plan Your Trip 4

Roman Forum (p44)

VOLOLIBERO/SHUTTERSTOCK ©

Explore Rome 37

Worth a Trip

Survival Guide 173

Special Features

Welcome to Rome

A heady mix of haunting ruins, awe-inspiring art and vibrant street life, Italy's hot-blooded capital is one of the world's most romantic and charismatic cities. Iconic monuments and priceless masterpieces recall its epic past while everyday life plays out on streets packed with colourful markets and old-school trattorias, chic boutiques and hidden cocktail bars. Visit once and you'll be hooked for life.

Fontana della Barcaccia and the Spanish Steps
ALEKANTON/SHUTTERSTOCK

Rome's Top Experiences

Shudder at the Colosseum's bloody history (p40)

Admire masterpieces in the Vatican Museums (p78)

Enjoy architectural perfection at the Pantheon (p58)

Marvel at the Borghese Gallery (p112)

VIACHESLAV LOPATIN/SHUTTERSTOCK ©

NICOLA FORENZA/SHUTTERSTOCK ©

SILVERFOX999/SHUTTERSTOCK ©

Ponder epic power at St Peter's Basilica (p84)

MISTERVLAD/SHUTTERSTOCK ©

Tour the Via Appia Antica (p154)

VALERIOMEI/SHUTTERSTOCK ©

Toss a coin in the Trevi Fountain (p98)

Relive the past in the Roman Forum (p44)

F8 STUDIO/SHUTTERSTOCK ©

ADISA/SHUTTERSTOCK ©

Watch the sunset at the Spanish Steps (p100)

Discover Palazzo Massimo alle Terme (p118)

Admire Basilica di Santa Maria in Trastevere (p160)

Explore Basilica di San Giovanni in Laterano (p134)

Dining Out

This is a city that lives to eat. Food feeds the Roman soul, and a social occasion would be nothing without it. Over recent decades, the restaurant scene has become increasingly sophisticated, but traditional no-frills trattorias still provide Rome's most memorable gastronomic experiences.

Roman Trattorias

The bedrock of the Roman food scene has long been the family-run trattorias that pepper the city's streets and piazzas. These simple eateries, often with rickety wooden tables and *nonna* (grandma) at the stove, have been feeding visitors for centuries and are still the best bet for no-nonsense Roman dishes such as *amatriciana* (a tomato sauce flavoured with *guanciale* – cured pig's cheek – and served with pasta, typically thick spaghetti called *bucatini*) or carbonara (*guanciale*, egg and salty *pecorino romano* cheese paired with spaghetti or rigatoni pasta tubes).

Street Food

Street food is hugely popular in Rome and recent years have seen a trend for gourmet fast food sweep the city. Alongside *pizza al taglio* (sliced pizza) joints and gelaterie, you'll find numerous places serving classic snacks such as *supplì* (fried rice balls with various fillings) and *fritti* (fried foods) with a modern twist.

Best Sliced Pizza

Bonci Pizzarium Pizza slices created by the master, Gabriele Bonci. (p92)

Forno Roscioli Thin and crispy, this is some of the best *pizza rossa* ('red' pizza with tomato) in Rome. (p69)

Forno di Campo de' Fiore Purveyors of the city's best *pizza bianca* ('white' pizza, with olive oil, rosemary and salt). (p72)

La Renella Historic bakery known for its bread, biscuits and pizza slices. (p167)

Casamano Dazzling flavour combinations on a perfect slow-risen base at Testaccio market.

COLORMAKER/SHUTTERSTOCK ©

Best Gelato

Gelateria del Teatro Around 40 choices of delicious ice cream, all made on site.

Gelateria dei Gracchi A taste of heaven in several locations across Rome. (p93)

Fior di Luna Great artisan ice cream in Trastevere. (p167)

Otaleg Superb handmade gelato using the freshest ingredients at this Trastevere favourite. (p167)

Best Traditional Roman

Flavio al Velavevodetto Classic *cucina romana* in a popular neighbourhood trattoria. (p145)

Felice a Testaccio A superb *cacio e pepe* as well as traditional Roman offal-based dishes. (p149)

Mordi e Vai Traditional Roman dishes turned street food, stuffed into panini at this Testaccio stall. (p150)

Trattoria Gallo Brillo A vintage trattoria dedicated to typical Roman staples. (p92)

Best Modern Roman

Il Sorpasso Fabulous updated takes on classic Roman dishes at this Prati hotspot. (p92)

Pianostrada Modern Roman dining with a strong emphasis on vegetables. (p69)

La Ciambella Set over the ancient Terme di Agrippa, the cuisine is unabashedly modern. (p70)

Rimessa Roscioli Modern Roman cuisine paired with exquisite local wines. (p69)

Top Tips for Eating Out

∘ In restaurants, it's standard to be given bread and charged for it whether you eat it or not.

∘ When tipping, leave a euro or two in pizzerias/trattorias; five to 10% is fine in smarter restaurants.

Bar Open

There's simply no city with better backdrops for a coffee or drink than Rome: you can sip espresso in historic cafes, claim piazza seating for an aperitivo (pre-dinner drink and snacks) or wander from wine bar to restaurant to late-night drinking den, getting happily lost down picturesque cobbled streets in the process.

Where to Drink

Options range from traditional cafes to old-school *enoteche* (wine bars), craft beer pubs and chic lounge bars serving *aperitivi* to the glitterati. Many cocktail bars also double as laid-back cafes by day – Trastevere has plenty of examples.

Clubbing

Rome's clubbing action, centred on Ostiense and Testaccio, caters to most tastes with DJs playing everything from lounge and jazz to dancehall and hip-hop. Clubs get busy after midnight, or even 2am.

Best Cafes

Caffè Sant'Eustachio Historic *centro storico* cafe serving exceptional coffee. (p72)

La Bottega del Caffè Terrace seating overlooking Monti's prettiest piazza; great coffee, too. (p127)

Barnum Cafe Laid-back *Friends*-style cafe with shabby-chic furniture and good coffee. (p63)

Antico Caffè Greco Located near the Spanish Steps, this 1760 charmer is Rome's oldest cafe. (pictured; p109)

Best Wine Bars

L'Angolo Divino Laid-back wine bar run by a sommelier with an interest in biodynamic wines. (p72)

Wine Concept Run by expert sommeliers, with an extensive list of Italian regional labels and European vintages. (p141)

Ai Tre Scalini Buzzing enoteca that feels as convivial as a pub. (p127)

La Mescita Neighbourhood natural wine bar in off-beat Garbatella. (p153)

Best Aperitivo

Il Goccetto Old-school *vino e olio* bar serving handsome meat and cheese platters. (p72)

Enoteca l'Antidoto Back-street Trastevere bar serving excellent cold cuts, cheeses and more. (p170)

ANDREAS SOLARO/AFP/GETTY IMAGES ©

Doppiozeroo Popular Ostiense address with impressive buffet choice. (p153)

Mescita Ferrara Delicious aperitivo in a sophisticated Trastevere wine bar. (p170)

Lettere Caffè The aperitivo spread at this inclusive Trastevere cafe is all-vegetarian. (p170)

Best Cocktail Bars

Club Derrière At the rear (get it?) of a trattoria, with top-notch cocktails. (p74)

Drink Kong Serious mixology at this neon-lit, Japanese-style Monti bar.

Terrazza Monti Sleek hotel rooftop bar that's a serene escape from the streets. (p127)

Ch 18 87 A secret Testaccio bar that mixes a mean Negroni. (p151)

Best Beer

Bar San Calisto Linger over cheep beer at this popular Trastevere hangout. (p169)

Ma Che Siete Venuti a Fà Pint-sized bar crammed with real-ale choices. (p169)

Open Baladin More than 40 beers on tap and up to 100 bottled brews. (p73)

Artisan Craft beers from Italy and overseas at this hipster haunt.

L'Oasi della Birra Much-loved Testaccio bar that is a true 'oasis of beer'. (p150)

Top Tip for Clubbers

Romans tend to dress up to go out, especially in the smarter clubs and bars in the *centro storico* (historic centre) and Testaccio. Over in Pigneto and San Lorenzo, the style is much more alternative.

History

For thousands of years Rome was at the centre of world events. First, as caput mundi (capital of the world), the glittering hub of the vast Roman Empire, and then as the seat of papal power. It was a city that counted – and this is writ large on its historic streets, where every palazzo, church and ancient ruin has a tale to tell.

Ancient Glories

Many of Rome's most thrilling monuments hark back to its golden age as the fearsome hub of the Roman Empire. The Colosseum, Pantheon, Roman Forum – these epic ruins all tell of past glories in a way that no textbook ever could.

Church Rule

For much of its history, the Church called the shots in Rome and many of the city's top sights are religious in origin. Early basilicas stand testament to the tenacity of the Church's founding fathers, while the masterpieces that litter the city's churches testify to the wealth and ambition of the Renaissance and baroque-era popes.

Layers of History

One of Rome's characteristic features is the way history literally rises from the ground. Over the centuries the city has undergone various transformations and with each one a new layer was added to the city's urban fabric. As a result, medieval churches stand over pagan temples and baroque piazzas sit atop Roman arenas.

Best Roman Relics

Colosseum Rome's iconic amphitheatre encapsulates all the drama of ancient Rome. (p26)

Pantheon This awe-inspiring temple has served as an architectural blueprint for millennia. (p58)

Terme di Caracalla The hulking remains of this baths complex are among Rome's most impressive. (pictured; p147)

Roman Forum The inspiring ruins of ancient Rome's showpiece city centre. (p44)

GIOVANNI RINALDI/SHUTTERSTOCK ©

Best Underground

Basilica di San Clemente
A medieval basilica set atop
a pagan temple and 1st-
century house. (p137)

Catacombs Via Appia Antica
is riddled with catacombs
where the early Christians
buried their dead.

**Le Domus Romane di
Palazzo Valentini** Excavated
ruins extend beneath a stately
16th-century mansion. (p105)

Best Churches

St Peter's Basilica The
Vatican's showpiece church
stands over St Peter's tomb.
(p84)

**Basilica di San Giovanni
in Laterano** The main
papal basilica until the 14th
century. (p134)

**Basilica di San Paolo
Fuori le Mura** Monumental
basilica on the site where St
Paul was buried. (p153)

Chiesa del Gesù Important
Jesuit church, home to
Ignatius Loyola for 12 years.
(p68)

Best Legendary Sites

Palatino Where the wolf
saved Romulus and Remus,
and Rome was founded in
753 BCE. (p51)

Bocca della Verità Tell a lie
and the 'Mouth of Truth' will
bite your hand off. (p54)

Tempietto del Bramante A
perfect Renaissance tomb
said to stand on the stop
where St Peter was cruci-
fied. (p166)

Worth a Trip: Ancient Rome's Port

Rome's answer to Pompeii, the **Area
Archeologica di Ostia Antica** (www.
ostiaantica.beniculturali.it) offers an insight
into ancient Rome's once-thriving port. To
get there, take the train from Stazione Porta
San Paolo (by Piramide metro station).

Art & Museums

Home to some of the world's greatest art, Rome is a visual feast. Its churches contain priceless masterpieces and its museums are laden with instantly recognisable works. From classical statues and Renaissance frescoes to baroque sculptures and futuristic paintings, the art on show spans almost 3000 years of artistic endeavour.

Classical Art

Rome's collection of ancient art – comprising sculpture, commemorative reliefs and mosaics – is unparalleled. The Vatican Museums and Capitoline Museums showcase the city's finest sculpture, but you'll also find superlative pieces at Palazzo Altemps and Palazzo Massimo alle Terme.

Renaissance

The Renaissance unleashed an artistic maelstrom in 16th-century Rome as Church patrons commissioned artists such as Michelangelo and Raphael to decorate the city's basilicas and palaces. Many celebrated frescoes date to this period, including Michelangelo's Sistine Chapel.

The Baroque

The baroque burst onto Rome's art scene in the early 17th century and was adopted by the Church as a propaganda tool in its battle against Reformation heresy. Works by the period's two leading artists – Gian Lorenzo Bernini and Caravaggio – adorn churches and museums across the city.

Best Museums

Vatican Museums The Sistine Chapel and Raphael Rooms headline at this spectacular museum complex. (p78)

Museo e Galleria Borghese Houses Rome's best baroque sculpture and some superlative Old Masters. (p112)

Capitoline Museums Ancient sculpture is the main draw at the world's oldest public museum. (pictured; p51)

Museo Nazionale Romano: Palazzo Massimo alle Terme Overlooked gem boasting fabulous Roman frescoes, sculpture and mosaics. (p118)

CHANCLOS/SHUTTERSTOCK ©

Palazzo Barberini Baroque palace laden with paintings by Caravaggio, Raphael, Hans Holbein, Pietro da Cortona et al. (p104)

Galleria Doria Pamphilj Lavish gallery full of major works by big-name Italian and Flemish artists. (p67)

Best Church Art

Sistine Chapel Michelangelo's frescoes are among the world's most famous works of art. (p78)

St Peter's Basilica Marvel at Michelangelo's *Pietà* and many other celebrated masterpieces. (p84)

Chiesa di San Luigi dei Francesi Baroque church boasting a trio of moody Caravaggio paintings. (p66)

Basilica di Santa Maria del Popolo Works by Caravaggio, Raphael and Bernini adorn this Renaissance church. (p104)

Basilica di Santa Maria in Trastevere Ancient basilica ablaze with golden apse mosaics. (p160)

Best Under-the-Radar Museums

Museo Nazionale Etrusco di Villa Giulia Showcases Italy's finest collection of Etruscan treasures. (p115)

Mercati di Traiano Museo dei Fori Imperiali Set in Trajan's towering 2nd century forum complex. (p26)

Centrale Montemartini A former power plant provides a stunning setting for wonderful ancient sculptures. (p153)

Top Tips for Culture Seekers

○ Most museums are closed on Mondays.

○ State museums are free for under-18s and discounted for EU nationals aged 18 to 25. Take ID as proof of age.

Responsible Travel

Follow these tips when you're in Rome to leave a lighter footprint, support local businesses and have a positive impact on communities.

Choose Sustainable Venues

Eat to support refugee integration The Gustamundo restaurant has operated in Via Giacinto de Vecchi Pieralice since 2017, hiring migrants and political refugees to promote integration.

Buy fair-trade, organic goods Visit the Sunday market Città dell'Altra Economia (cittadellaltraeconomia. org) in the Testaccio neighbourhood – one of the first spaces in Europe dedicated to the promotion of an alternative economy.

Look out for Slow Food products The Slow Food organisation (www. slowfoodroma.it) promotes projects that protect genuine traditions and local ecosystems.

Give Back

Learn about social struggles Visit Città dell'Utopia (www. lacittadellutopia.org) – a volunteer-run organisation at Via Valeriano 3F – to participate in talks, movie screenings, games, and courses on topics such as gender inequality, the environment and social inclusion.

Buy produce cultivated on lands confiscated from the Mafia Look out for the Libera Terra label when shopping for groceries at places such as NaturaSì.

Donate or volunteer to help the homeless Binario95 (www.binario95.it), located by Termini, has been providing a home for the homeless for the past 20 years. Do your part by donating or participating in volunteering events.

Learn More

Learn about less-visited neighbourhoods Go beyond the centre and explore the culture of Garbatella on a walking tour by Unexpected Rome, run by local architect and certified guide Valeria Castiello.

Discover the city's multicultural character Learn about the rich history of Esquilino by joining a walk by Migrantours.

Support Locals

Shop at markets Support small vendors while enjoying the lively atmosphere of one of many markets. Testaccio, Porta Portese, Esquilino, San Lorenzo – it's your choice.

Search for unique souvenirs at bottegas Whether it's handmade shoes or a

ROSSHELEN/SHUTTERSTOCK ©

carved picture frame, you'll never be disappointed by the quality at Roman artisans' workshops.

Eat farm-to-table vegetarian dishes Reduce your footprint by eating traditional dishes made with hyperlocal ingredients.

Leave a Small Footprint

Reduce food waste Download the app Too Good to Go to get unsold food from eateries at a discounted price.

Shop at zero-waste stores Buy packaging-free groceries at Negozio Leggero (Via Chiabrera 80) or Resto Sfuso (Via Santa Maria Ausiliatrice 68).

Drink plastic-free Visit fontanelle.org to locate a nearby drinking fountain (the city has 5000) to refill your bottle.

Climate Change & Travel

It's impossible to ignore the impact we have when travelling, and the importance of making changes where we can.

Lonely Planet urges all travellers to engage with their travel carbon footprint. There are carbon calculators online that allow travellers to estimate the carbon emissions generated by their journey; try resurgence.org/resources/carbon-calculator.html. Many airlines and booking sites offer travellers the option of offsetting the impact of greenhouse gas emissions by contributing to climate-friendly initiatives around the world.

We continue to offset the carbon footprint of all Lonely Planet staff travel, while recognising this is a mitigation more than a solution.

Treasure Hunt

REPORT/SHUTTERSTOCK ©

Rome has a huge array of specialist shops, fashion boutiques and artisans' workshops, with a particularly impressive portfolio of food, clothing and accessory boutiques. Many of these businesses are family owned, having been passed down through the generations. Others have grown from their modest origins into global brands.

Best Fashion

Bomba Family-operated atelier and boutique selling gorgeous clothing. (p110)

Gente An emporium-style, multi-label boutique. (p110)

Tina Sondergaard Retro-inspired dresses in a bijou Monti boutique. (p129)

LOL Beautifully curated selection of subtly elegant womenswear in Monti. (p128)

Best Artisanal

Confetteria Moriondo & Gariglio Divine chocolates crafted from 19th-century recipes. (p74)

Del Giudice Sleek leather goods handcrafted in Rome. (p75)

Perlei Artisan-made jewellery with a modernist aesthetic. (p129)

Antica Manifattura Cappelli A 1930s milliners studio in Prati. (p95)

Best Gourmet Food

Antica Caciara Trasteverina Wonderful, century-old deli in Trastevere. (p170)

Confetteria Moriondo & Gariglio A 19th-century shop specialising in handmade chocolates. (p74)

Salumeria Roscioli Byword for foodie excellence, with mouth-watering delicacies (pictured).

Volpetti Bulging with delicious delicacies, with notably helpful staff. (p151)

Eataly Ostiense foodie superstore. (p153)

How To Be a Savvy Shopper

○ Many city-centre shops are closed on Monday morning.

○ Winter sales run from early January to mid-February, and summer sales from July to early September.

Architecture

Boasting ancient ruins, Renaissance basilicas, baroque churches and fascist palazzi (mansions), Rome's architectural legacy is unparalleled. Michelangelo, Bramante, Borromini and Bernini have all stamped their genius on its remarkable cityscape, while in recent years several top architects have completed projects in the city.

XNICK/SHUTTERSTOCK ©

Best Ancient Sites

Colosseum Rome's iconic arena showcases Roman architecture on an unprecedented scale. (pictured; p26)

Pantheon The dome finds perfect form atop this revolutionary structure. (p58)

Terme di Caracalla These looming ruins hint at the sophistication of ancient building techniques. (p147)

Mercati di Traiano Museo dei Fori Imperiali A towering model of 2nd-century civic engineering. (p26)

Via Appia Antica The archetypal Roman road lined with Roman tombs and ruined villas.

Best Early Basilicas

Basilica di San Giovanni in Laterano Its design set the style for basilicas to follow. (p134)

Basilica di Santa Maria Maggiore The only one of Rome's four patriarchal basilicas to retain its original layout. (p123)

Basilica di Santa Sabina A 5th-century church built with columns from the Temple of Juno. (p148)

Best Renaissance Styling

St Peter's Basilica An amalgamation of designs, styles and plans capped by Michelangelo's extraordinary dome. (p84)

Palazzo Farnese A stunning example of a classical Renaissance palace. (p68)

Piazza del Campidoglio Michelangelo's piazza is a show-stopping example of Renaissance town-planning. (p52)

Tempietto del Bramante One of the most harmonious buildings of the High Renaissance. (p166)

Best Baroque Gems

St Peter's Square Bernini designed the Vatican's focal square to funnel believers into St Peter's Basilica.

Piazza Navona With a Borromini church and a Bernini fountain, this celebrated square is a model of baroque beauty. (p66)

Culture

The Romans have long been passionate about culture. Ever since crowds flocked to the Colosseum for gladiatorial games, the locals have enjoyed a good show, and cultural events draw knowledgeable and enthusiastic audiences. Rome has everything from opera to hip-hop and Shakespearean drama to avant-garde installations.

KIEV.VICTOR/SHUTTERSTOCK ©

Best Classical Venues

Auditorium Parco della Musica Great acoustics, top international musicians and multiple concert halls. (p115)

Teatro dell'Opera di Roma Red velvet and gilt interior for Rome's opera and dance companies. (p128)

Terme di Caracalla Wonderful outdoor setting for summer opera and ballet. (pictured; p150)

Teatro Argentina One of Rome's oldest theatres showcasing great classics as well as avant garde works. (p74)

Best Live Music

Blackmarket Hall Two bars filled with vintage sofas, great for eclectic, mainly acoustic, live music. (p128)

Caffè Letterario A basement bookshop doubling as a lounge with live music.

ConteStaccio Free live music on the Testaccio clubbing strip.

Fonclea Pub Prati pub with live gigs featuring everything from rock to doo-wop. (p95)

Best Jazz

Alexanderplatz Rome's foremost jazz club stages international and local musicians. (p94)

Big Mama An atmospheric Trastevere venue for jazz, blues, funk, soul and R&B. (p170)

Gregory's Jazz Club This smooth venue near the Spanish Steps is popular with local musicians. (p109)

Top Tips for Tickets

○ Check listings on www.060608.it, www. romeing.it, www.inromenow.com.

○ For tickets, try **Vivaticket** (www.vivaticket.it) or **Orbis Servizi** (www.boxofficelazio.it).

Tours

OLGA SERDYUKOVA ITALIA/SHUTTERSTOCK ©

Taking a guided tour is an excellent way of seeing a lot in a short time or investigating a sight in depth. On foot, bike, golf cart, scooter or bus, these tours show the city from a new perspective. In high season, book tours in advance to avoid disappointment.

Best Walking Tours

Understanding Rome (www.understandingrome. com) Architectural historian, Agnes Crawford, leads dynamic and insightful tours of big-hitting sites as well as secret treasures.

A Friend in Rome (https://afriendinrome.it) Silvia Prosperi and her team offer private tours covering the main historic centre, plus areas outside the capital.

The Tour Guy (https:// thetourguy.com) Packages, led by English-speaking experts, include skip-the-line visits to the city's top sights and foodie tours of Trastevere.

Best Bike, Golf Cart or Scooter Tours

Red Bicycle (www. theredbicycle.org) A cycle outfit offering a range of cycling tours in and around the city.

Bici & Baci (www.bicibaci. com; pictured) Runs daily bike tours taking in the main historical sites. Also tours on vintage Vespas, classic Fiat 500 cars and three-wheeled Ape Calessinos.

Roman Roads Tours (https://romanroadstours. com) A pioneering provider of environmentally friendly electric golf cart tours that zip around the main sites, sparing your shoe leather.

Best Bus Tours

Open Bus Vatican & Rome (www. omniavaticanrome.org/it/ cards/il-servizio-open-bus-vatican-rome) A hop-on, hop-off bus with stops near main sights, including St Peter's Basilica, Piazza Navona and the Colosseum.

Best Food Tours

Katie Parla (https:// katieparla.com) Exciting guided food walks delving into Rome's markets and kitchens. Cooking classes and wine tastings are also possible.

Elizabeth Minchilli (www. elizabethminchilli.com) Food writer Elizabeth and her daughter Sophie lead small groups to all the best markets and delis in the city.

For Free

Rome is an expensive city, but you don't have to break the bank to enjoy it. A surprising number of its big sights are free, and it costs nothing to stroll the historic streets, piazzas and parks, basking in their extraordinary beauty.

ONLY FABRIZIO/SHUTTERSTOCK ©

Best Free Art

St Peter's Basilica Michelangelo's *Pietà* is just one of the masterpieces on display. (p84)

Basilica di San Pietro in Vincoli Feast your eyes on Michelangelo's muscular Moses. (p125)

Chiesa di San Luigi dei Francesi Caravaggio's St Matthew cycle is the big drawcard here. (p66)

Basilica di Santa Maria del Popolo Boasts two Caravaggios and frescoes by Pinturicchio. (p104)

Best Piazzas & Parks

Piazza Navona A colourful cast of street artists animate this stunning piazza. (p66)

Piazza di Spagna Rome's most beautiful staircase provides the perfect frame for souvenir photos. (p26)

Villa Borghese Rome's central park is ideal for picnics. (pictured; p26)

Piazza del Popolo A grandiose piazza with art-filled churches, an Egyptian obelisk and a pretty urban walk up Pincio Hill. (p105)

Via Appia Antica Rome's 'queen of roads' flanked by tombs and pines is free to walk or cycle.

Best Free Monuments

Pantheon There's no charge to enter this temple turned church. (p58)

Trevi Fountain Free, unless you throw a coin in to ensure your return to Rome. (p98)

Vittoriano Rome's most high-vis monument offers stunning views. (p26)

Top Tips for Money Savers

∘ State-run museums are free the first Sunday of the month between October and March. The Vatican Museums are *gratis* every last Sunday.

∘ Fill up with water from drinking fountains known as *nasoni* (big noses).

Under the Radar Rome

ESSEVU/SHUTTERSTOCK ©

From the Colosseum to the Sistine Chapel, Rome's historic sites are among the most visited in Italy. That means crowds and the risk of over-tourism, particularly in peak periods. To avoid the queues and discover another side of Rome, set your sights on the city's lesser-known gems and neighbourhoods.

Best Alternative Neighbourhoods

Testaccio Once-proletarian Testaccio is a foodie hotspot with popular trattorias and a busy neighbourhood market.

Ostiense Against a backdrop of street art and industrial landmarks, Ostiense harbours hot clubs and hip bars as well as several cultural gems.

Garbatella Full of colour, Garbatella is known for its eclectic architecture, lush courtyards and eye-catching street murals.

EUR In Rome's southern reaches, EUR is a world apart with its muscular modern architecture.

San Lorenzo Hang out with the students in left-field San Lorenzo, packed with craft-beer bars, grungy music venues and basement dives.

Best Off-Track Sights

Cimitero Acattolico per gli Stranieri Pay homage to romantic poets and socialist thinkers at this peaceful Testaccio oasis. (p147)

Museo Capitoline Centrale Montemartini Ancient sculpture sidles up to heavy industrial machinery at this decommissioned power station in Ostiense. (p153)

Chiesa di Santo Stefano Rotondo A secluded church on the Celio hosting a chilling cycle of 16th-century frescoes. (pictured; p137)

Basilica di Santa Prassede Be bowled over by dazzling Byzantine mosaics at this easy-to-miss Esquilino church. (p124)

Transport Tidbit

Several of Rome's most interesting neighbourhoods can be accessed on line B of the metro. These include Testaccio, Ostiense, Garbatella and EUR.

For Kids

Despite a reputation as a highbrow cultural destination, Rome has a lot to offer kids. Child-specific sights might be thin on the ground, but if you know where to go, there's plenty to keep the little 'uns occupied and parents happy.

TRAVNIKOVSTUDIO/SHUTTERSTOCK ©

Best Museums & Sites for Kids

Colosseum (www.parcocolosseo.it) Kids and adults alike will be blown away by the chance to imagine gladiators, wild animals and crowds at ancient Rome's greatest stadium.

Villa Borghese Rent bikes, four-person surreys, or even take a rowboat out on the lake to explore Rome's most beautiful park. Rome's zoo, **Bioparco** (www.bioparco.it), with 200 species from five continents, is also located here.

Eye Spy Rome is full of monuments and viewpoints that make for fun treasure hunts. Find Egyptian obelisks and animal-themed fountains, like the turtles on the **Fon-**

tana delle Tartarughe, or spot the best views at the **Spanish Steps**, the **Fori Imperiali** (www.mercatiditraiano.it) or atop the **Vittoriano** (https://vittoriano.beniculturali.it/it).

Pizza & Ice-cream Plot your own or book a kid-friendly food tour and discover the city's best pizza slices or ice-cream flavours.

Bici & Baci (www.bicibaci.com) Take a thrilling tour on vintage Vespas or funky three-wheeled Ape Calessinos; or squeeze into a tiny classic Fiat 500.

Explora – Museo dei Bambini di Roma (www.mdbr.it) Rome's only dedicated kids' museum, Explora is aimed at the under-12s. Outside there's also a free play park.

Al Sogno (www.alsogno.com) This store is a wonderland of puppets, Pinocchios, trolls, fairies and stuffed animals.

Money Savers For Families

○ Under-18s get in free at state-run museums; city-run museums are free for under-sixes and discounted for six- to 25-year-olds.

○ Under-10s travel free on public transport.

LGBTIQ+

GENNARO LEONARDI PHOTOS/SHUTTERSTOCK ©

Rome has a thriving, if low-key, gay scene. There are relatively few queer-only venues, but the Colosseum end of Via di San Giovanni in Laterano is a favourite hangout and many clubs host regular gay and lesbian nights. Outside town, there are a couple of popular gay beaches at Ostia: Settimo Cielo and the Oasi Naturista Capocotta.

Best Events

Roma Pride (www.romapride.it) Rome's annual Gay Pride parade is the city's biggest celebration of the LGBTIQ+ community. It takes place in June and the parade commences in Piazza della Reppublica and is followed by a host of other events and dance parties.

Best Venues

Coming Out (www.comingout.it) On warm evenings, with lively crowds on the street and the Colosseum as a backdrop, there are few finer places to sip a drink than this friendly gay bar. It's open all day, but is at its best in the evening when the atmosphere heats up, the cocktails kick in

and the karaoke and speed dating get under way.

L'Alibi Gay-friendly L'Alibi is one of Rome's best known clubs, hosting regular parties and serving up a mash of house, hip hop, Latino, pop and dance music to a young, mixed crowd. It can get pretty steamy inside, particularly on packed weekend nights, but you can grab a mouthful of air on the spacious summer terrace.

Via di San Giovanni in Laterano Steps from the Colosseum, this bar-lined street is the beating heart of Rome's LGBTIQ+ scene.

Muccassassina (www.muccassassina.com) A notorious LGBTIQ+ dance party conceived by Francesco Simonetti (killingcow DJ) and friends in 1991. It is held every Friday, from mid-October to June, at the Qube disco on Via di Portonaccio 212.

Top Tip for Venue Entry

Most gay venues require you to have an Arcigay membership card. These cost €10 from the **Arcigay** (www.arcigayroma.it) headquarters in Testaccio or any venue that requires one.

Four Perfect Days

Day 1

Start the day at the **Colosseum** (p40), Rome's huge gladiatorial arena. Then head to the **Palatino** (p51) to poke around ancient ruins, before descending into the **Roman Forum** (pictured; p44).

After lunch at **Alle Carette** (p125), stop by **Piazza del Campidoglio** (p52) and the **Capitoline Museums** (p51), where you'll find some sensational ancient sculpture. Done there, enjoy views from the **Vittoriano** (p52) before pressing on to the **Pantheon** (p58) and **Piazza Navona** (p66).

Spend the evening in the *centro storico* (historic centre): dine at **La Ciambella** (p70), then chat over coffee at **Caffè Sant'Eustachio** (p72).

Day 2

First up on day two are the **Vatican Museums** (p78). Once you've blown your mind on the Sistine Chapel and the myriad other masterpieces, complete your Vatican tour at **St Peter's Basilica** (p84).

After lunching on sliced pizza at **Bonci Pizzarium** (p92), jump on the metro to **Piazza di Spagna** (p100). Snap a classic souvenir photograph on the famous **Spanish Steps** (p100), then push on to the **Trevi Fountain** (pictured; p98).

Finish the day off with a fabulous cocktail in **Hassler Bar** (p108) or with dinner at **Colline Emiliane** (p106).

Day 3

ANNA PAKUTINA/SHUTTERSTOCK ©

Day three starts with a trip to the **Museo e Galleria Borghese** (p112) to marvel at amazing baroque sculpture and Renaissance masterpieces. Afterwards, take a stroll through Rome's central park, **Villa Borghese** (p115).

In the afternoon, press on to **Piazza del Popolo** (p105) to catch a couple of Caravaggio's masterpieces at the **Basilica di Santa Maria del Popolo** (pictured; p104). Next, dedicate some time to browsing the flagship stores and designer boutiques in the streets off **Via del Corso**.

Over the river, the picture-perfect **Trastevere** neighbourhood bursts with life in the evening. Hotspots include **Enoteca L'Antidoto** (p170), a laid-back wine bar, and local favourite, **Bar San Calisto** (p169).

Day 4

MODLS84/SHUTTERSTOCK ©

On day four, venture out to **Via Appia Antica** (p154) where you can go underground in the **catacombs** (p156) and poke around ancient ruins at the **Villa di Massenzio** (pictured; p157).

When you're done, head back to Stazione Termini and the nearby **Museo Nazionale Romano: Palazzo Massimo alle Terme** (p118) for some classical sculpture and stunning mosaics. Then, drop by the **Basilica di Santa Maria Maggiore** (p123) and **Basilica di San Pietro in Vincoli** (p125), home to Michelangelo's Moses sculpture. Finish up with some shopping in the fashionable **Monti** district.

Stay put in Monti in the evening with dinner at **La Barrique** (p126), then pick a bar or cafe to see out the day.

Need to Know

For detailed information, see Survival Guide (p173)

Currency
Euro (€)

Language
Italian

Visas
Generally not required for stays of up to 90 days.

Money
ATMs are widespread. Major credit cards are widely accepted but some smaller businesses might prefer cash.

Mobile Phones
Local SIM cards can be used in European phones and in unlocked Australian and US phones. Other phones must be set to roaming.

Time
Western European Time (GMT/UTC plus one hour)

Tipping
Not necessary, but round the bill up in pizzerias/trattorias or leave a euro or two; five to 10% is fine in smarter restaurants.

Daily Budget

Budget: Less than €120

Dorm bed: €25–50

Double room in a budget hotel: €60–130

Pizza plus beer: €15

Midrange: €120–300

Double room in a hotel: €100–200

Local restaurant meal: €25–45

Admission to Vatican Museums: €17

Roma Pass, a 72-hour card covering museum entry and public transport: €52

Top end: More than €300

Double room in a four- or five-star hotel: €200 plus

Top restaurant dinner: €45–180

Opera ticket: €17–150

City-centre taxi ride: €10–15

Auditorium concert tickets: €20–90

Advance Planning

Two months before Book high-season accommodation.

One month before Check for concerts at auditorium.com. Book tickets for Colosseum tours, private tours of the Vatican and visits to the Museo e Galleria Borghese and Palazzo Farnese.

One to two weeks before Reserve tickets for the pope's weekly audience at St Peter's.

Few days before Reserve tables at top restaurants. Book tickets for the Vatican Museums and Colosseum (advisable to avoid queues).

Arriving in Rome

Most people arrive by plane at one of Rome's two airports: Leonardo da Vinci, better known as Fiumicino, or Ciampino, the hub for Ryanair. Trains serve Rome's main station, Stazione Termini, from a number of European destinations, including Paris (about 15 hours), as well as cities across Italy.

✈ From Leonardo da Vinci (Fiumicino) Airport

Located 30km west of the city centre.

Leonardo Express trains To Stazione Termini; 6.38am to 11.38pm; €14.

FL1 trains Slower trains to Trastevere, Ostiense and Tiburtina stations; 5.57am to 10.42pm; €8.

Buses To Stazione Termini; 6.05am to 12.40am; €6-7.

Airport-to-hotel shuttles From €22 per person.

Taxis Fixed fare to within the Aurelian walls €50.

✈ From Ciampino Airport

Situated 15km southeast of the city centre.

Buses To Stazione Termini; 8.15am to 12.15am; €6.

Airport-to-hotel shuttles Per person €25.

Taxis Fixed fare to within the Aurelian walls €31.

🚌 From Stazione Termini

Near the city centre. Airport buses & trains, and international trains, arrive at Stazione Termini. From there, continue by bus, metro or taxi.

Getting Around

Public transport includes buses, trams, metro and suburban trains. The main hub is Stazione Termini. Tickets, which come in various forms, are valid for all forms of transport. Children under 10 travel free.

Ⓜ Metro

The metro is quicker than surface transport, but the network is limited. Two main lines serve the centre, A (orange) and B (blue), crossing at Stazione Termini. Trains run between 5.30am and 11.30pm (to 1.30am Fridays and Saturdays).

🚌 Bus

Most routes pass through Stazione Termini. Buses run from approximately 5.30am until midnight, with limited services throughout the night.

🚲 Cycling & Electric Scooters

Cycle paths are expanding in Rome and even getting special cycle lanes. There are plans for 150km of paths in coming years. E-bikes can be rented on apps like Lime and Helbiz.

Electric scooters are an increasingly popular way to get around. Rent them via apps like Bird, Dott, Lime, Helbiz or Wind. Prices start at €0.15 per minute.

🚶 Walk

Walking is the best way of getting around the *centro storico* (historic centre).

Rome Neighbourhoods

Vatican City, Borgo & Prati (p77)
Feast on extravagant art in the monumental Vatican and excellent food in neighbouring Prati.

Centro Storico (p57)
Rome's historic centre is the capital's thumping heart – a heady warren of famous squares and tangled lanes, galleries, restaurants and bars.

Trastevere & Gianicolo (p159)
Trastevere's medieval streets heave with kicking bars and eateries. The Gianicolo offers to-die-for panoramas.

Vatican
Museums ◉

Spanish Steps & Piazza di Spagna ◉

◉
St Peter's Basilica

Trevi Fountain ◉

Pantheon ◉

Basilica di ◉
Santa Maria
in Trastevere

Aventino & Testaccio (p143)
Ideal for a romantic getaway, hilltop Aventino rises above Testaccio, famous for its nose-to-tail cooking and thumping nightlife.

Tridente, Trevi & the Quirinale (p97)

Debonair, touristy area boasting a presidential palace, Rome's most famous fountain, designer boutiques and swish bars.

Museo e Galleria Borghese ⊙

Museo Nazionale Romano: Palazzo Massimo alle Terme ⊙

Monti & Esquilino (p117)

Boutiques and wine bars abound in Monti, while Esquilino offers multiculturalism and several must-see museums and churches.

Roman Forum ⊙

⊙ *Colosseum*

⊙ *Basilica di San Giovanni in Laterano*

Ancient Rome (p39)

Rome's ancient core is a beautiful area of evocative ruins, improbable legends, soaring pine trees and panoramic views.

⊙ *Via Appia Antica*

San Giovanni & Celio (p133)

Explore medieval churches and escape the tourist crowds in residential San Giovanni and on the leafy Celio hill.

Explore
Rome

Worth a Trip 👓

City's Walking Tours 🥾

Colosseum (p40) ESB PROFESSIONAL/SHUTTERSTOCK ©

Explore
Ancient Rome

In a city of extraordinary beauty, Rome's ancient heart stands out. It's here you'll find the great icons of the city's past: the Colosseum, the Palatino, the forums and the Campidoglio (Capitoline Hill), the historic home of the Capitoline Museums. Touristy by day, it's quiet at night with few after-hours attractions.

The Short List

○ **Colosseum (p40)** *Getting your first glimpse of Rome's iconic amphitheatre.*

○ **Palatino (p51)** *Exploring the haunting ruins of the Palatine Hill, ancient Rome's birthplace and most exclusive neighbourhood.*

○ **Capitoline Museums (p51)** *Going face to face with centuries of awe-inspiring art at the world's oldest public museums.*

○ **Roman Forum (p44)** *Exploring the basilicas, temples and triumphal arches of what was once the nerve centre of the Roman Empire.*

○ **Vittoriano (p52)** *Surveying the city spread out beneath you from atop this colossal marble extravaganza.*

Getting There & Around

🚌 Buses 40, 64, 87, 170, 916 and H to Piazza Venezia. Bus 87 runs along Via dei Fori Imperiali between the Colosseum and Vittoriano.

Ⓜ Line B for the Colosseum (Colosseo) and Circo Massimo. If taking the metro at Termini, follow signs for Line B 'direzione Laurentina'.

Neighbourhood Map on p50

Roman Forum (p44) MO WU/SHUTTERSTOCK ©

Top Experience 📷

Shudder at the Colosseum's Bloody History

⊙ MAP P50, D4

www.parcocolosseo.it

An awesome, spine-tingling sight, the Colosseum is the most thrilling of Rome's ancient monuments. It was here that gladiators met in fierce combat and condemned prisoners fought off wild beasts in front of baying, bloodthirsty crowds. Two thousand years on and it's Italy's top tourist attraction, drawing more than seven million visitors a year.

History

The emperor Vespasian (r 69–79 CE) originally commissioned the amphitheatre in 72 CE in the grounds of Nero's vast Domus Aurea complex. He never lived to see it finished, though, and it was completed by his son and successor Titus (r 79–81) in 80 CE. To mark its inauguration, Titus held games that lasted 100 days and nights, during which some 5000 animals were slaughtered. Trajan (r 98–117) later topped this, holding a marathon 117-day killing spree involving 9000 gladiators and 10,000 animals.

The 50,000-seat arena was Rome's first, and greatest, permanent amphitheatre. For some five centuries it was used to stage lavish, crowd-pleasing spectacles to mark important anniversaries or military victories. Gladiatorial combat was eventually outlawed in the 5th century but wild animal shows continued until the mid-6th century.

Following the fall of the Roman Empire, the Colosseum was largely abandoned. It was used as a fortress by the powerful Frangipani family in the 12th century and later plundered of its precious building materials. Travertine and marble stripped from the Colosseum were used to decorate a number of Rome's notable buildings, including Palazzo Venezia, Palazzo Barberini and Palazzo Cancelleria.

More recently, pollution and vibrations caused by traffic have taken a toll. To help counter this, it was given a major cleanup between 2014 and 2016, the first in its 2000-year history, as part of an ongoing €25 million restoration project sponsored by the luxury shoemaker Tod's. In addition, in 2021, the Italian government pledged €10 million for the installation of a new, retractable floor that will enable the Colosseum to be used once again for large-scale cultural spectacles.

★ Top Tips

○ Visit early morning or late afternoon to avoid the crowds.

○ If queues are long, get your ticket at the Palatino, about 250m away at Via di San Gregorio 30.

○ Other queue-jumping tips: book tickets online at www. coopculture.it (plus €2 booking fee), get the Roma Pass or SUPER ticket, or join a tour.

○ Basic full-price admission tickets can be pre-printed; reduced/free/tour tickets must be picked up on site.

○ Between July and October, magical evening tours (€25) can be booked online.

✕ Take a Break

Avoid the rip-off restaurants in the vicinity. Instead head to the area east of the Colosseum for superior pizza and *fritti* at Alle Carrette (p125).

The Exterior

The outer walls have three levels of arches, framed by decorative columns topped by capitals of the Ionic (at the bottom), Doric and Corinthian (at the top) orders. They were originally covered in travertine, and marble statues filled the niches on the 2nd and 3rd storeys. The upper level, punctuated with windows and slender Corinthian pilasters, had supports for 240 masts that held the awning over the arena, shielding the spectators from sun and rain. The 80 entrance arches, known as *vomitoria,* allowed the spectators to enter and be seated in a matter of minutes.

The Seating

The *cavea,* or spectator seating, was divided into three tiers: magistrates and senior officials sat in the lowest tier, wealthy citizens in the middle and the plebs in the highest tier. Women (except for vestal virgins) were relegated to the cheapest sections at the top. Tickets were numbered and spectators were assigned a precise seat in a specific sector – in 2015, restorers uncovered traces of red numerals on the arches, indicating how the sectors were numbered.

The podium, a broad terrace in front of the tiers of seats, was reserved for the emperor, senators and VIPs.

The top three rings, known collectively as the Belvedere, can also be visited on guided tours.

Colosseum interior

Colosseum Curiosities

The Name

The arena was originally known as the Flavian Amphitheatre (Anfiteatro di Flavio) after Vespasian's family name. And while it was Rome's most famous arena, it wasn't the biggest – the Circo Massimo could hold up to 250,000 people. The name Colosseum, when introduced in the Middle Ages, wasn't a reference to its size but to the Colosso di Nerone, a giant statue of Nero that stood nearby.

Gladiatorial Games

Games staged here usually involved gladiators fighting wild animals or each other. But contrary to Hollywood folklore, bouts rarely ended in death, as the games' sponsor was required to pay compensation to a gladiator's owner if the gladiator died in action.

The Arena

The stadium originally had a wooden floor covered in sand – *harena* in Latin, hence the word 'arena' – to prevent combatants from slipping and to soak up spilt blood.

Trapdoors led down to the hypogeum, a subterranean labyrinth of corridors, cages and lifts used to transport animals and scenography up to the arena's sandy floor.

Hypogeum

The hypogeum served as the stadium's backstage area. It was here that stage sets were prepared and combatants, both human and animal, would gather before showtime. Gladiators entered from the nearby Ludus Magnus (gladiator school) via an underground corridor, whilst a second tunnel, the Passaggio di Commodo (Passage of Commodus), allowed the emperor to arrive without having to pass through the crowds.

To hoist people, animals and scenery up to the arena, the hypogeum was equipped with a sophisticated network of 80 winch-operated lifts, all controlled by a single pulley system.

Visits to the hypogeum are by guided tour only. These can be booked online at www.coopculture.it. Not all tickets include this area, so check what's included in the ticket price.

Top Experience 📷

Relive the Past in the Roman Forum

The Roman Forum was ancient Rome's centre-piece, a grandiose district of temples, basilicas and vibrant public spaces. Nowadays it's a collection of impressive, if sketchily labelled, ruins that can leave you drained and confused. A good guide (or audio guide) will certainly help you here, conjuring stories of legendary figures and endless scheming as you step through ancient Rome's epic and bloody history.

◉ MAP P50, B3

Foro Romano

www.parcocolosseo.it

Via Sacra & Tempio di Giulio Cesare

Entering from Largo della Salara Vecchia, a path leads down to **Via Sacra**, the Forum's main thoroughfare, and the **Tempio di Giulio Cesare**, aka Tempio del Divo Giulio. Built by Augustus in 29 BCE, this marks the spot where Caesar was cremated after his assassination in 44 BCE.

Curia

Heading right up Via Sacra brings you to the **Curia**, the original seat of the Roman Senate. This barn-like construction was rebuilt on various occasions and what you see today is a 1937 reconstruction of how it looked in the reign of Diocletian (r 284–305).

Arco di Settimio Severo & Rostri

At the end of Via Sacra, the 23m-high **Arco di Settimio Severo** is dedicated to the eponymous emperor and his two sons, Caracalla and Geta. Built in 203 CE, it commemorates Roman victories over the Parthians.

Close by are the remains of the **Rostri**, an elaborate podium where local politicos would harangue the market crowds.

Facing the Rostri, the **Colonna di Foca** rises above what was once the Forum's main square, **Piazza del Foro**.

Tempio di Saturno

Eight granite columns are all that survive of the **Tempio di Saturno**, one of the Forum's landmark sights. Inaugurated in 497 BCE and subsequently rebuilt in the 1st century, it was an important temple that doubled as the state treasury.

Tempio di Castore e Polluce

In the centre of the Forum, three columns remain from the 5th-century BCE **Tempio di Castore e Polluce**, dedicated to the heavenly twins Castor and Pollux.

★ Top Tips

○ Get grandstand views of the Forum from the Palatino and Campidoglio.

○ Visit first thing in the morning or late afternoon; crowds are worst between 11am and 2pm.

○ In summer it gets very hot and there's little shade, so take a hat and plenty of water. Comfortable shoes are a must.

○ If you're caught short, there are toilets by the Chiesa di Santa Maria Antiqua.

○ To enter the Chiesa di Santa Maria Antiqua, Rampa di Domiziano and Tempio di Romolo, you'll need the SUPER ticket (p54).

○ Downloadable audio guides are available on the Parco Colosseo app.

✖ Take a Break

Take a coffee break at Terrazza Caffarelli (p55) on the Capitoline Museums' panoramic rooftop.

Alternatively, Osteria Circo (p54) serves excellent Roman cuisine.

Chiesa di Santa Maria Antiqua

The 6th-century **Chiesa di Santa Maria Antiqua** is the oldest and most important Christian site on the forum. It's a treasure trove of early Christian art containing exquisite 6th- to 9th-century frescoes, and one of the oldest icons in existence.

Casa delle Vestali

The **Casa delle Vestali** (House of the Vestal Virgins) was the home of the virgins who tended the flame in the adjoining **Tempio di Vesta**. At its centre is a rectangular grassy space lined with a string of statues, now mostly headless, depicting the Vestals.

Basilica di Massenzio

The **Basilica di Massenzio** is the largest building on the Forum. Started by Maxentius and finished by Constantine in 315, it originally measured 100m by 65m, roughly three times its current area.

Arco di Tito

Said to be the inspiration for Paris' Arc de Triomphe, the **Arco di Tito** was built by Domitian in 81 CE to celebrate his brother Titus' military victories in Judea and the 70 CE sack of Jerusalem. In the past, Roman Jews would avoid passing under the arch, which is considered the historical symbol of the beginning of the Jewish Diaspora.

Roman Forum

100 m

Via Cavour

N

Via del Tempio della Pace

Via del Colosseo

Via Francesca

Via del Colosseo

Via dei Fori Imperiali

Via dei Fori Imperiali

Largo C Ricci

Largo della Salara Vecchia

Entrance

Basilica di Massenzio

Via Sacra

Arco di Tito

Entrance

Via della Salara Vecchia

Tempio di Giulio Cesare

Casa delle Vestali

Orti Farnesiani

Via della Curia

Curia

Via Sacra

Tempio di Castore e Polluce

Tempio di Vesta

Colonna di Foca

Piazza del Foro

Chiesa di Santa Maria Antiqua

Via dei Tulliano

Rostri

Arco di Settimio Severo

Vicus Tuscus

Via di San Pietro in Carcere

Entrance

Tempio di Saturno

Via del Foro Romano

Via dei Foragi

Piazza del Campidoglio

Via della Consolazione

Via dei Fienili

Walking Tour 🥾

Emperors' Footsteps

Follow in the footsteps of Rome's legendary emperors on this walk around the best of the city's ancient treasures. Established in 27 BCE, the Roman Empire grew to become the Western world's first dominant superpower. At the peak of its power, in about 100 CE, it extended from Britain to north Africa, and from Syria to Spain.

Walk Facts

Start Colosseum; metro Colosseo

End Vittoriano; bus Piazza Venezia

Length 2km; at least three hours

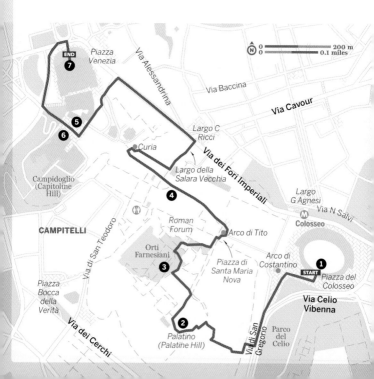

❶ Colosseum

More than any other monument, it's the **Colosseum** (p40) that symbolises the power of ancient Rome. A spectacular feat of engineering, the 50,000-seat stadium was inaugurated by Emperor Titus in 80 CE with a bloodthirsty bout of games that lasted 100 days.

❷ Palatino

A short walk from the Colosseum, the **Palatino** (p51) was ancient Rome's most sought-after neighbourhood, site of the emperor's palace and home to the cream of imperial society. The evocative ruins are confusing but their grandeur gives a sense of the luxurious life of ancient VIPs.

❸ Orti Farnesiani

Covering a vast area of the Palatino is the magical 16th-century **Orti Farnesiani** (p51), one of Europe's earliest botanical gardens. Established by Cardinal Alesssandro Farnese, it is planted with exotic specimens and has a balcony commanding breathtaking views over the Roman Forum.

❹ Roman Forum

Coming down from the Palatino, you'll enter the **Roman Forum** (p44) near the Arco di Tito, one of Rome's triumphal arches. The Forum was the empire's social and civic nerve centre. The vestal virgins lived here and senators debated matters of state in the Curia.

❺ Piazza del Campidoglio

Exit the Forum at Largo della Salara Vecchia and head up to the Michelangelo-designed **Piazza del Campidoglio** (p52). This piazza sits atop the Campidoglio (Capitoline Hill), one of the seven hills on which Rome was founded and the spiritual heart of the ancient city.

❻ Capitoline Museums

Flanking Piazza del Campidoglio are two stately *palazzi* (mansions) housing the **Capitoline Museums** (p51). These, the world's oldest public museums, boast an important picture gallery and a collection of classical sculpture that includes the *Lupa Capitolina*, a bronze wolf standing over her suckling wards, Romulus and Remus.

❼ Vittoriano

From the Campidoglio, pop next door to the mountain of white marble that is the **Vittoriano** (p52). No emperor ever walked here, but it's worth taking the panoramic lift to the top, from where you can see the whole of Rome laid out beneath you.

✗ Take a Break

Hidden in the Capitoline Museums but accessible by its own entrance, **Terrazza Caffarelli** (p55) is a refined spot for a coffee.

Via del Corso

A

1

Via Cesare Battisti

5 ⊙ Palazzo Venezia

Piazza di Venezia

Piazza
San Marco

2

Piazza
d'Aracoeli

⊙**4**
Vittoriano

Capitoline
Museums
12
⊙**2** Piazza del Campidoglio
⊙**3**

3

Via di
Monte
Caprino

Via Consolazione

CAMPITELLI

4

⊗**11**

Piazza
Bocca
della
Verità

Via del Velabro

Piazza di
Sant'Anastasia

5 ⊙ Bocca della
9 Verità

Via della
Greca

Via del Cerchi

13
⊗**10**

Clivio del Publico

Via del Circo Massimo

6
Parco
Savello

B

Villa
Colonna

Via IV
Novembre

Colonna
Traiana

⊙**6**
Mercati di
Traiano Museo
dei Fori Imperiali

Imperial
Forums

⊙**7** Via Alessandrina

Via dei Fori Imperiali

Largo
C Ricci

Largo della
Salara Vecchia

Basilica dei SS ⊙**8**
Cosma e Damiano

Roman ⊙
Forum

Orti
Farnesiani

Piazza di
Santa Maria
Nova

Via Sacra

Vigna
Barberini

⊙ Palatino
1

Circo
Massimo

Via dei Cerchi

C

Largo
Angelicum

Via del Serpenti

Piazza
Madonna
dei Monti

Via della Madonna dei Monti

Via Cavour

Via del Colosseo

Via dei Fori Imperiali ℹ

Largo G
Agnesi
Via N Salvi

Ⓜ
Colosseo

Colosseum
⊙

Arco di
Costantino Piazza del
Colosseo

Via Celio Vibenna

Via di San Gregorio

Parco
del
Celio

Viale del Parco del Celio

Clivo di Scauro

D

For reviews see	
⊙ Top Experiences	p40
⊙ Sights	p51
⊗ Eating	p54
Ⓠ Drinking	p55

Via Baccina

Via del Tor
de' Conti

Via degli Annibaldi

Sights

Palatino

ARCHAEOLOGICAL SITE

1 ◉ MAP P50, C5

Sandwiched between the Roman Forum and the Circo Massimo, the Palatine Hill is home to towering pine trees, majestic ruins and unforgettable views. This is where Romulus supposedly founded the city in 753 BCE and where Rome's patricians lived in palatial luxury. Look out for the **stadio** (stadium), the ruins of the **Domus Flavia** (imperial palace), and grandstand views over the Roman Forum from the **Orti Farnesiani**. Visiting the houses of Augustus and Livia is a highlight – book ahead. (Palatine Hill; www.parcocolosseo.it)

Capitoline Museums

MUSEUM

2 ◉ MAP P50, A3

Dating from 1471, the Capitoline Museums are the world's oldest public museums. The collection of classical sculpture is one of Italy's finest, boasting works such as the iconic *Lupa Capitolina* (Capitoline Wolf), a life-size bronze of a she-wolf suckling Romulus and Remus, and the *Galata morente* (Dying Gaul), a moving depiction of a dying warrior. There's also a for-midable gallery with masterpieces by the likes of Titian, Tintoretto, Rubens and Caravaggio. Ticket prices increase when there's a temporary exhibition on. (www. museicapitolini.org)

Lupa Capitolina, Capitoline Museums

Local Tips: Ancient Views

Palatine Hill The terrace overlooking the Roman Forum offers one of the best views in the world. Once on the Palatine Hill, follow signs for the Farnese Gardens and keep going to the northeast corner. You'll be rewarded with a sweeping panorama taking in the Colosseum, the Forum, and everything to the mountains beyond. Working out how the higgledy-piggledy jumble of buildings that made up the Forum fits together is a lot easier from up above.

Colosseum If entering the Forum at the Arch of Titus entrance, bear right at the arch before going down the stairs, turn to face the Colosseum, and keep walking for the best views from the terrace of the ruined Temple of Venus.

The Forum In 1839 Turner painted his view of 'Modern Rome' as seen from Capitoline Hill. Today it is one of the very best views of the Forum, doesn't require a ticket, and can be admired at any time of day or night. I especially recommend late afternoon as the setting sun casts a brilliant light over the remains of 25 centuries of human endeavour. From the Piazza del Campidoglio, take the right-hand path under the mini Bridge of Sighs to the junction of via del Campidoglio and via del Monte Tarpeo.

 By Agnes Crawford, architectural historian and tour guide, @understandingrome

Piazza del Campidoglio
PIAZZA

3 ◉ MAP P50, A3

This hilltop piazza, designed by Michelangelo in 1538, is one of Rome's most beautiful squares. There are several approaches but the most dramatic is the graceful **Cordonata** (Piazza d'Aracoeli) staircase, which leads up from Piazza d'Aracoeli. The piazza is flanked by **Palazzo Nuovo** and **Palazzo dei Conservatori**, together home to the Capitoline Museums and Palazzo Senatorio, Rome's historic city hall. In the centre is a copy of an equestrian **statue of Marcus Aurelius**.

Vittoriano
MONUMENT

4 ◉ MAP P50, A2

Love it or loathe it (as many Romans do), you can't ignore the Vittoriano (aka the Altare della Patria, or Altar of the Fatherland), the colossal mountain of white marble that towers over Piazza Venezia. It was built at the turn of the 20th century to honour Italy's first king, Vittorio Emanuele II, who's immortalised in its vast equestrian statue. (https://vittoriano.beniculturali.it/it)

Palazzo Venezia

MUSEUM

5 ◉ MAP P50, A1

Built between 1455 and 1464, Palazzo Venezia was the first of Rome's great Renaissance palaces. For centuries it was the embassy of the Venetian Republic – hence its name – but it's most readily associated with Mussolini, who had his office here and famously made speeches from the balcony of the Sala del Mappamondo (Globe Room). Nowadays, it's home to the **Museo Nazionale del Palazzo Venezia** and its eclectic collection of Byzantine and early Renaissance paintings, ceramics, bronze figures, weaponry and armour. (www.museopalazzovenezia. beniculturali.it)

Mercati di Traiano Museo dei Fori Imperiali

MUSEUM

6 ◉ MAP P50, B2

This striking museum showcases the **Mercati di Traiano** (Trajan's Markets), the emperor Trajan's towering 2nd-century complex, while also providing a fascinating introduction to the Imperial Forums with multimedia displays, explanatory panels and a smattering of archaeological artefacts. Sculptures, friezes and the occasional bust are set out in rooms opening onto what was once the Great Hall. But more than the exhibits, the real highlight here is the chance to explore the vast structure, which historians believe housed the forums' administrative offices. (www.mercatiditraiano.it)

Imperial Forums

ARCHAEOLOGICAL SITE

7 ◉ MAP P50, B2

The forums of Trajan, Augustus, Nerva and Caesar are known collectively as the Imperial Forums. They were largely buried when Mussolini bulldozed Via dei Fori Imperiali through the area in 1933, but excavations have since unearthed much of them. The standout sights are the Mercati di Traiano (p53) and the **Colonna Traiana**, with its incredible spiral frieze depicting Rome's victories against Dacia (roughly modern Romania).

Basilica dei SS Cosma e Damiano

BASILICA

8 ◉ MAP P50, C3

Backing onto the Roman Forum, this 6th-century basilica incorporates parts of the Foro di Vespasiano and Tempio di Romolo, visible at the end of the nave. However, the main reason to visit is to admire its fabulous 6th-century apse mosaic depicting Peter and Paul presenting saints Cosma, Damiano, Theodorus and Pope Felix IV to Christ. Also worth a look is the

Ticket Lowdown

To visit the Palatino and Roman Forum's internal sites, you'll need to buy a Full Experience ticket (€22) and plan carefully. The ticket, valid for two consecutive days, covers the Colosseum, the Hypogeum, Roman Forum and Palatino. A cheaper, SUPER ticket (€16) is valid for a day and gives you access to everything but the Colosseum. **Coopculture** (www.coopculture.it) offers a fantastic Colosseum by Night tour (between May and October) of the Arena and the Hypogeum. Download the new **ParCoColosseo app** which allows you to book tickets, informs you of all the rules and includes six different routes to explore.

18th-century Neapolitan **presepe** (nativity scene) in a room off the salmon-orange 17th-century cloister. (www.cosmadamiano.com)

Bocca della Verità   MONUMENT

9 MAP P50, A5

A bearded face carved into a giant marble disc, the Bocca della Verità is one of Rome's most popular curiosities. Legend has it that if you put your hand in the mouth and tell a lie, the *bocca* (mouth) will slam shut and bite it off. The mouth, which was originally part of a fountain, or possibly an ancient manhole cover, now lives in the portico of the **Chiesa di Santa Maria in Cosmedin**, a handsome medieval church. (Mouth of Truth)

Eating

Osteria Circo   LAZIO €€

10 ✖ MAP P50, B5

This warm-hearted osteria is a surprising find near Circo Massimo. It has a vaulted interior and a well-stocked bar that lends the rustic dining room a cosy feel. It focuses on traditional Roman dishes and flavours. The rosemary focaccia, *cacio e pepe* croquettes, artichokes in creamed pecorino and the *spaghettone ajo, ojo e pepperoncino* (olive oil, garlic and chilli pepper) are all delicious. (https://osteriacirco.it)

47 Circus Roof Garden   RISTORANTE €€€

11 ✖ MAP P50, A4

With the Aventino hill rising in the background, the rooftop restaurant of the Forty Seven Hotel sets a romantic scene for contemporary Mediterranean cuisine. Seafood features heavily on the seasonal menu, appearing in creative antipasti, with pasta and in main courses. (www.47circusroofgarden.com)

Bocca della Verità

Drinking

Terrazza Caffarelli

CAFE

12  MAP P50, A3

On the 2nd floor of the Capitoline Museums and with a terrace commanding views over the city's domes and rooftops, this cafe has waiter service on the terrace and a cheaper self-service cafeteria inside. You don't need a museum ticket to reach the cafe, which can be accessed from Piazzale Caffarelli as well as from inside the museum itself.

0,75

BAR

13 MAP P50, B5

This welcoming bar overlooking the Circo Massimo is good for a lingering evening drink, an *aperitivo* or a casual meal (mains €6 to €17). It's a friendly place with a laid-back vibe, an international crowd, an attractive wood-beamed look and cool tunes. (www.075roma.com)

Explore

Centro Storico

A tightly packed tangle of cobbled alleyways, Renaissance palaces, ancient ruins and baroque piazzas, the historic centre is the Rome many come to see. Its theatrical streets teem with boutiques, cafes, trattorias and stylish bars, while market traders and street artists work its vibrant squares. You'll also find a host of monuments, museums and churches, many laden with priceless artworks.

The Short List

○ **Pantheon (p58)** Stepping into this architecturally perfect temple and feeling the same sense of awe that the ancients must have felt 2000 years ago.

○ **Piazza Navona (p66)** Admiring the beauty of this baroque piazza with its flamboyant fountains and elegant chiesa.

○ **Galleria Doria Pamphilj (p67)** Browsing the artistic treasures at this fabulous private gallery.

○ **Chiesa di San Luigi dei Francesi (p66)** Clocking three Caravaggio masterpieces at this historic church.

○ **Historic Streets** Strolling the area's atmospheric lanes, taking in the colourful street life and hidden nooks.

Getting There & Around

🚌 A whole fleet serves the area from Termini, including 40 and 64, which both stop at Largo di Torre Argentina and continue down Corso Vittorio Emanuele II.

Ⓜ The neighbourhood is walkable from Barberini, Spagna and Flaminio stations, all on line A.

🚊 Tram 8 runs from Piazza Venezia to Trastevere.

Neighbourhood Map on p64

Pantheon (p58) MAPICS/SHUTTERSTOCK ©

Top Experience 📷

Enjoy Architectural Perfection at the Pantheon

 MAP P64, D3

www.pantheonroma.com

A striking 2000-year-old temple, now a church, the Pantheon is Rome's best-preserved ancient monument and one of the most influential buildings in the Western world. Its greying, pockmarked exterior might look its age, but inside it's a different story. It's a unique and exhilarating experience to pass through its vast bronze doors and gaze up at the largest unreinforced concrete dome ever built.

History

In its current form, the Pantheon dates to around 125 CE. It was built by the emperor Hadrian over an earlier temple constructed by Marcus Agrippa in 27 BCE. Hadrian's temple was dedicated to the classical gods – hence the name Pantheon, a derivation of the Greek words *pan* (all) and *theos* (god) – but in 608 CE it was consecrated as a Christian church. It's now officially known as the Basilica di Santa Maria ad Martyres.

Exterior

The monumental entrance portico consists of sixteen 11.8m-high columns supporting a triangular pediment. Behind the columns, two 20-tonne bronze doors – 16th-century restorations of the originals – give onto the central rotunda.

Interior

With light streaming in through the oculus (the 8.7m-diameter hole in the dome), the cylindrical marble-clad interior seems vast. Opposite the entrance is the church's main altar, while to the left are the tombs of the artist Raphael, King Umberto I and Margherita of Savoy. Over on the opposite side of the rotunda is the tomb of King Vittorio Emanuele II.

The Dome

The Pantheon's dome, considered the Romans' greatest architectural achievement, was the largest dome in the world until the 15th century when Brunelleschi beat it with his Florentine cupola. Its harmonious appearance is due to a precisely calibrated symmetry – its diameter is equal to the building's interior height of 43.4m. At its centre, the oculus plays a vital structural role by absorbing and redistributing the structure's huge tensile forces.

★ Top Tips

o The Pantheon is a working church; mass is celebrated at 5pm on Saturdays and 10.30am on Sundays.

o Visit around midday to see a beam of sunlight stream in through the oculus.

o Look down as well as up – the sloping marble floor has 22 drainage holes for the rain falling through the oculus.

o Return after dark for amazing views of the building set against the ink-blue night sky.

o Audio guides are available inside for €8.50.

o At the weekend and on public holidays you must prebook your visit (and audio guide) online one day in advance.

✗ Take a Break

The streets around the Pantheon are thick with trattorias and cafes. For an uplifting espresso, try La Casa del Caffè Tazza d'Oro (p73).

Walking Tour 🥾

Piazzas of Rome

Rome's tightly packed historic centre boasts some of the city's most celebrated piazzas, and several beautiful but lesser known squares. Each has its own character but together they encapsulate much of the city's beauty, history and drama. Take this tour to discover the best of them and enjoy the area's vibrant street life.

Walk Facts

Start Largo di Torre Argentina; bus Largo di Torre Argentina

Finish Piazza Farnese; bus Corso Vittorio Emanuele II

Length 2.4km; three hours

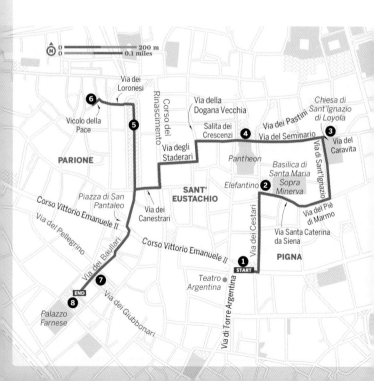

❶ Largo di Torre Argentina

Start off in Largo di Torre Argentina, set around the ruins of four Republic-era temples. On the western side, the **Teatro Argentina** (p74), sits near the site where Julius Caesar was assassinated.

❷ Piazza della Minerva

Head along Via dei Cestari until you come to Piazza della Minerva and the **Elefantino**, a cute sculpture of a chubby elephant carrying a 6th-century Egyptian obelisk. The adjacent Gothic **Basilica di Santa Maria Sopra Minerva** (p66) boasts a beautiful star-studded ceiling, fabulous frescoes and the tomb of Renaissance painter Fra Angelico.

❸ Piazza di Sant'Ignazio Loyola

Strike off down Via Santa Caterina da Siena, then take Via del Piè di Marmo and Via di Sant'Ignazio to reach the stage-set 18th-century Piazza di Sant'Ignazio Loyola. Overlooking the piazza, the **Chiesa di Sant'Ignazio di Loyola** (p67) features a dramatically swirling trompe l'oeil ceiling fresco sucking St Ignatius into a heavenly vortex.

❹ Piazza della Rotonda

A short stroll down Via del Seminario brings you to the Piazza della Rotonda, where the **Pantheon** (p58) needs no introduction. Rome's best-preserved ancient building, with its epic portico and dome, is one of the city's iconic sights.

❺ Piazza Navona

From the Pantheon, follow the signs to **Piazza Navona** (p66), central Rome's great showpiece square. Here, among the throng, you can compare the two giants of Roman baroque – Gian Lorenzo Bernini, creator of the Fontana dei Quattro Fiumi, and Francesco Borromini, author of the Chiesa di Sant'Agnese in Agone.

❻ Chiesa di Santa Maria della Pace

A few steps west, down Vicolo della Pace, is the charming, miniature **Chiesa di Santa Maria della Pace** (www.chiostrodelbramante.it). Pietro da Cortona designed the elegant semicircular facade while Raphael decorated the **Chigi Chapel** with a fresco of *Sibyls and Angels* (c 1515).

❼ Campo de' Fiori

Head south and cross Corso Vittorio Emanuele II to reach **Campo de' Fiori** (p72), a focal point of Roman life. By day, this noisy square stages a colourful market; at night it plays host to a lively drinking scene.

❽ Piazza Farnese

Just beyond the Campo, Piazza Farnese is a refined square overlooked by the Renaissance **Palazzo Farnese** (p68). This magnificent *palazzo*, now home to the French embassy, boasts superb frescoes, said to rival those of the Sistine Chapel. Visits are by guided tour only (€12).

Walking Tour 🚶

A Day Out in the Centro Storico

Rome's historic centre casts a powerful spell. But it's not just visitors who fall for its romantic piazzas, suggestive lanes and streetside cafes. Away from the tourist spotlight, locals love to spend time here, shopping, unwinding over a drink, taking in an exhibition or simply hanging out with friends.

Walk Facts

Start I Dolci di Nonna Vicenza; bus Arenula/Cairoli

End Piazza Ponte di Sant'Angelo; bus Lungotevere Tor di Nona

Length 1.6km; six hours

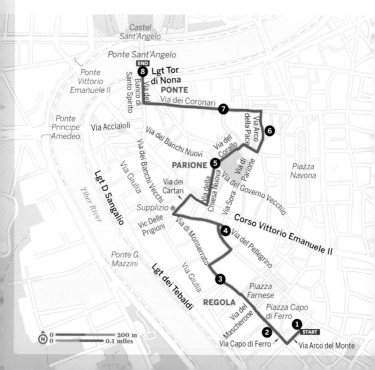

❶ Donna Vicenza

For an indulgent breakfast, seek out **I Dolci di Nonna Vicenza** (www.dolcinonnavicenza.it). An outpost of one of Sicily's top *pasticcerie*, it serves delicious cannoli stuffed with pistachio cream.

❷ Puzzle Over an Optical Illusion

Turn right down Vicolo dei Venti to seek out the Secret Garden in Cardinal Spada's art-filled **Palazzo Spada** (www.galleriaspada.beniculturali.it). Here you'll find an intriguing optical illusion created by tortured genius Borromini in 1653 – a long colonnade leading to a courtyard which appears three times its actual length. The apparently life-size statue of Mars at the end is a miniature 60cm tall.

❸ Via di Monserrato

Turn left, pass Palazzo Farnese and walk up **Via di Monserrato**, the *centro storico's* chicest street lined with artisan ateliers. Look out for bag designer Halaby, Chez Dede concept store and L'Archivio di Monserrato, the fashion boutique of Soledad Twombly.

❹ Savour a light lunch

Hop across a street and stop for a light lunch at **Barnum Cafe** (www.barnumroma.com) where you can order excellent Caesar salads and plates of homemade pasta. Or grab one of **Supplizio's** (www.supplizioroma.it) famous fried rice balls.

❺ Vintage-shop hop on Via del Governo Vecchio

Head up Vicolo Savelli to **Via del Governo Vecchio**, the quintessential *centro storico* street. Once lined with government offices, it is now packed with vintage shops and bars. Check out Omero e Cecilia and Vestiti Usati Cinzia.

❻ An Exhibition at the Chiostro del Bramante

Take Via di Parione to the Chiesa di Santa Maria della Pace. Down the right-hand side you'll find **Bramante's cloister** (p61), a masterpiece of high Renaissance architecture. It now provides a stunning setting for modern-art exhibitions.

❼ Via dei Coronari

A few steps further north is **Via dei Coronari**, where rosary beads (*corone*) were once hawked and where prelates housed their mistresses. Antique shops abound, alongside boutiques such as textile atelier Lisa Corti, Roman perfumier Essenzialmente Laura and artisanal Gelateria del Teatro.

❽ Ponte Sant'Angelo

Follow Via dei Coronari to Piazza di Ponte, overlooking the River Tiber. The piazza was the site of capital executions and victims' bodies once decorated the **Ponte Sant'Angelo**. Now, the bridge is guarded by two colossal statues of St Peter (left) and St Paul (right) and 10 angels carrying symbols of the Passion.

Centro Storico

200 m
0.1 miles

Tiber River

Lgt Tor di Nona

Lgt Marzio

Ponte Umberto I

Piazza Nicosia

Piazza di San Silvestro

Via del Corso

Via del Corso

Palazzo Chigi

Piazza Colonna

Palazzo di Montecitorio

Piazza di Montecitorio

Piazza del Parlamento

Via di Campo Marzio

Via dei Prefetti

Via degli Uffici del Vicario

Via della Stelletta

Club Derrière

Via della Maddalena

Via delle Murate

Minghetti Tourist Information

Via delle Coppelle

Piazza delle Cinque Lune

Via dei Portoghesi

Via dell'Orso

Via di Monte Brianzo

Via dei Soldati

Museo Nazionale Romano: Palazzo Altemps

Piazza Tor Sanguigna

Via G Zanardelli

Via dei Coronari

Piazza Lacellotti

Vic delle Vacche

Via del Corallo

Bar del Fico

Via dei Parione

Via di Sora

Via del Governo Vecchio

PARIONE

Jerry Thomas Project (50m)

Corso Vittorio Emanuele II

Via del Pellegrino

Argot

Piazza di San Pantaleo

Piazza della Cancelleria

Via di San Pantaleo

Piazza di Sant'Andrea della Valle

Via dei Canestrari

Piazza Navona

Corso del Rinascimento

Via Melone

Via del Teatro Valle

Via Monterone

Chiesa di San Luigi dei Francesi

Via Santa Maria dell'Anima

Largo Febo

Via della Scrofa

Basilica di Sant'Agostino

Via del Salvatore

Largo G Toniolo

Via della Dogana Vecchia

Via del Pantheon

Via Giustiniani

Salita dei Crescenzi

Via Sant'Eustachio

Via di Torre Argentina

Piazza delle Colonnelle

Via degli Orfani

Via dei Pastini

Piazza della Rotonda

Pantheon

Piazza della Minerva

Basilica di Santa Maria Sopra Minerva

Via dei Cestari

Via della Minerva

Via del Gesù

PIGNA

Piazza della Pigna

Piazza di Pietra

Via di Pietra

Piazza di Sant'Ignazio

Chiesa di Sant'Ignazio di Loyola

Via di Sant'Ignazio

Via della Caravita

Via Lata

Galleria Doria Pamphilj

Via della Gatta

Piazza Grazioli

Via del Piè di Marmo

Points:
- 1 Piazza Navona
- 2 Palazzo Altemps
- 3 Basilica di Sant'Agostino
- 4 Via del Salvatore
- 5 Basilica di Santa Maria Sopra Minerva
- 6 Chiesa di Sant'Ignazio di Loyola
- 7 Galleria Doria Pamphilj
- 13 Via della Scrofa
- 14
- 16
- 19
- 20
- 23
- 24 Piazza delle Colonnelle
- 26
- 27
- 29 Via delle Coppelle
- 30 Club Derrière
- 31

Centro Storico

Piazza Venezia

Piazza di San Marco

Piazza d'Aracoeli

Via del Teatro di Marcello

Vic Jungario

Via Petroselli

Via del Plebiscito

Chiesa del Gesù

Piazza del Gesù

Via di San Marco

Via d'Aracoeli

Via delle Botteghe Oscure

Via M Caetani

Via de' Funari

Via D'elfini

Piazza di Campitelli

Via Montanara

Via del Foro Piscario

Teatro di Marcello

SANT' ANGELO

Via del Portico d'Ottavia

Jewish Ghetto

Via Catalana

Isola del Cinema

Museo Ebraico di Roma

Ponte Fabricio

Isola Tiberina

Ponte Cestio

Largo di Torre Argentina

Via di Torre Argentina

Via Florida

Boccione

Ba'Ghetto

Via del Tempio

Via dei Falegnami

Piazza Costaguti

Via Santa Maria del Pianto

Via del Sudario

Via dei Barbieri

Via di Sant'Anna

Largo Arenula

Lgt de' Cenci

Yotvata

Via Arenula

Via San Bartolomeo dei Vaccinari

Lgt degli Anguillara

Lgt Raphaello Sanzio

Via dei Chiavari

Via dei Giubbonari

Via degli Specchi

Piazza B Cairoli

Ponte Garibaldi

Lgt dei Vallati

Piazza del Teatro di Pompeo

Forno

Campo de' Fiori & Mercato di Campo de' Fiori

Piazza del Biscione

Largo dei Librari

Via dei Balestrari

Via dei Cappellari

Via dei Baullari

Via del Pellegrino

Piazza Trinità dei Pellegrini

Via Capo di Ferro

Vic delle Grotte

Via delle Zoccolette

Via del Conservatorio

Lgt dei Tebaldi

Piazza Farnese

Palazzo Farnese

Via di Monserrato

Via dei Farnesi

Via Giulia

Ponte Sisto

Piazza Trilussa

Lgt della Farnesina

Tiber River

25
15
21
22
12
11
17
9
10
18
28
8

For reviews see

◉	Top Experiences	p58
⊙	Sights	p66
✖	Eating	p68
🍸	Drinking	p72
✿	Entertainment	p74
🛍	Shopping	p74

A B C D E F

1 2 3 4 5 6 7 8

Sights

Piazza Navona
1 ◉ MAP P64, B3   PIAZZA

With its showy fountains, baroque *palazzi* and colourful cast of street artists, hawkers and tourists, Piazza Navona is Rome's showcase square. Built over the 1st-century **Stadio di Domiziano** (www.stadiodomiziano. com), it was paved over in the 15th century and for almost 300 years hosted the city's main market. Its centrepiece is Bernini's **Fontana dei Quattro Fiumi** (Fountain of the Four Rivers).

Museo Nazionale Romano: Palazzo Altemps
2 ◉ MAP P64, C2   MUSEUM

This beautiful late-15th-century *palazzo* houses the Museo Nazionale Romano's formidable collection of classical sculptures.

Many pieces, including the dramatic *Galata suicida* (Gaul's Suicide), come from the celebrated collection of Cardinal Ludovico Ludovisi. Note, the combined ticket (€12 instead of €8) also gives you access to Diocletian's Baths (p124) and the fabulous frescoes in Palazzo Massimo alle Terme (p118) and is valid for a week. (www.museonazionaleromano. beniculturali.it)

Basilica di Sant'Agostino
3 ◉ MAP P64, C2   BASILICA

The plain facade of this early Renaissance church gives no indication of the impressive art inside. The most famous work is Caravaggio's *Madonna dei Pellegrini* (Madonna of the Pilgrims; 1604–06), in the first chapel on the left, but you'll also find Raphael's muscular *Profeta Isaia* (Prophet Isaiah, 1512) and a much-venerated sculpture by Jacopo Sansovino.

Chiesa di San Luigi dei Francesi
4 ◉ MAP P64, C3   CHURCH

Church to Rome's French community since 1589, this opulent baroque *chiesa* is home to a celebrated trio of Caravaggio paintings: the *Vocazione di San Matteo* (The Calling of Saint Matthew), the *Martirio di San Matteo* (The Martyrdom of Saint Matthew) and *San Matteo e l'angelo* (Saint Matthew and the Angel), known collectively as the St Matthew cycle. Find them in the Cappella Contarelli to the left of the main altar. (http://saintlouis-rome.net)

Basilica di Santa Maria Sopra Minerva
5 ◉ MAP P64, E4   BASILICA

Built on the site of three pagan temples, including one dedicated to the goddess Minerva, this Dominican basilica is Rome's only Gothic church with a soaring lapis-coloured ceiling studded with stars. Superb Renaissance frescoes by Filippino Lippi decorate the Cappella Carafa, to the right of the altar, and pious painter Fra' Angelico is buried here alongside St Catherine of Siena and two Medici popes. (www.santamariasopraminerva.it)

Chiesa di Sant'Ignazio di Loyola
CHURCH

6 ⊙ MAP P64, E3

This important Jesuit church boasts a Carlo Maderno facade and two celebrated *trompe l'œil* frescoes by Andrea Pozzo (1642–1709). One depicts a fake dome, while the other, in the nave, shows St Ignatius Loyola being welcomed into paradise. Thanks to Pozzo's virtuoso use of perspective, a mass of figures, led by St Ignatius, appears to float heavenwards past soaring columns and arches. (https://santignazio.gesuiti.it)

Galleria Doria Pamphilj
GALLERY

7 ⊙ MAP P64, F4

One of Rome's richest private art collections is housed in the austere Palazzo Doria Pamphilj. Masterpieces abound with works by Raphael, Tintoretto, Titian, Caravaggio, Bernini and Velázquez, as well as several Flemish masters, but the undisputed star is Velázquez' portrait of Pope Innocent X. When Innocent X saw it, he gasped, 'too real!' The audio guide, narrated by

Fontana dei Quatrro Fiumi

Jonathan Pamphilj, brings the place alive. (www.doriapamphilj.it)

Chiesa del Gesù
CHURCH

8 MAP P64, E5

Rome's most important Jesuit church is a treasure trove of baroque art. Headline works include a swirling vault fresco by Giovanni Battista Gaulli (aka Il Baciccia) and Andrea del Pozzo's opulent tomb for Ignatius Loyola, the Spanish soldier and saint who founded the Jesuits in 1540. St Ignatius lived in the church from 1544 until his death in 1556 and you can visit his private rooms to the right of the church. (www.chiesadelgesu.org)

Cinematic Island

Connected to the Jewish Ghetto and Trastevere by the Cestio (44 BCE) and Fabricio (62 BCE) bridges, the ship-shaped **Isola Tiberina** floats mysteriously in the River Tiber. Between June and September, it's the location for the **Isola del Cinema** (Map p64, D8; www.isoladelcinema.com), the largest open-air cinema festival in Rome featuring 80 nights of screenings alongside an array of Q&As, masterclasses and interviews. Expect an interesting roster of independent films, documentaries and international hits, some shown in their original language.

Palazzo Farnese
HISTORIC BUILDING

9 MAP P64, B5

Home to the French embassy, this Renaissance *palazzo*, one of Rome's finest, was started in 1514 by Antonio da Sangallo the Younger, continued by Michelangelo and finished by Giacomo della Porta. Inside, it boasts frescoes by Annibale and Agostino Carracci that are said by some to rival Michelangelo's in the Sistine Chapel. The highlight, painted between 1597 and 1608, is the monumental ceiling fresco *Amori degli Dei* (The Loves of the Gods).

Visits to the *palazzo* are by 45-minute guided tour (in English, French and Italian), for which you'll need to book at least a week in advance. Photo ID is required and children under 10 are not admitted. (https://visite-palazzofarnese.it)

Eating

Osteria La Quercia
LAZIO €€

10 MAP P64, B6

This elegant restaurant hides in plain sight beside a quaint piazza not far from Campo de' Fiori. The limited menu focuses on Lazio classics and sources ingredients from small-scale producers. Courgette flowers, salt cod croquettes, meatballs prepared in a saltimbocca style all are full of flavour. Ask your server for a wine suggestion from the well-stocked cellar. (www.osterialaquercia.com)

Worth a Trip: Jewish Ghetto

Rome's **Jewish Ghetto** (Map p64, D7) is an atmospheric neighbourhood. It is centred around Rome's main synagogue with its distinctive square dome and adjoining **museum** (Jewish Museum of Rome; Map p64, D7; www.museoebraico.roma.it) chronicling Rome's Jewish history.

The community is one of the oldest in Europe, dating back to the 2nd century BCE when the Jews of Judea and Samaria sought Rome's protection against Hellenistic aggression. But as the population grew, so too did prejudice and in 1555 Pope Paul IV passed a law confining Rome's Jews to live separated in this walled quarter.

Ironically, this confinement ensured the survival of Jewish cultural identity. In particular, the strict adherence to *kashrut* (religious food laws) resulted in a distinct Judeo-Roman cuisine of which the emblematic dish is *carciofo alla giuda* (fried artichokes). As *kashrut* prohibits the consumption of dairy and meat together, restaurants serve either one or the other. **Yotvata** (Map p64, C7; www.yotvata.it) is a traditional milk restaurant, serving kosher cheeses besides fried fish and vegetables, while **Ba'Ghetto** (Map p64, D7) serves kosher meat. For dessert, the sour cherry and ricotta cake at **Boccione** (Map p64, D6) bakery is famous.

Rimessa Roscioli
BISTRO €€€

11 MAP P64, B7

An offshoot of the Roscioli empire, Rimessa is geared to wine lovers: quality drops from all over Italy crowd the shelves, and the affable sommeliers know their craft. The food is equally impressive, *cucina romana* (Roman cuisine) executed with a modern sensibility. Come for a curated wine-and-food tasting or order à la carte. Booking is essential.

Nearby you'll find its other branches: an excellent bakery,

Forno Roscioli (www.anticofornoroscioli.it), serving Roman pizza slices, and top-notch deli-restaurant **Salumeria Roscioli** (www.salumeriaroscioli.com).

Pianostrada
BISTRO €€

12 MAP P64, B7

This contemporary bistro is adorned with vintage and designer furnishings and has a lovely rear courtyard. Reserve ahead for dinner, or settle at the bar and enjoy views of the chefs at work. The cuisine is creative

Local Tips: Busking Wisdom

I'm Brazilian by birth but was adopted and grew up in Rome.

I've been a busker for years and my top spot is Castel Sant'Angelo. The Foro Imperiali is also a good place for buskers, but the acoustics at the castle are better for a singer like me. People also like to hang-out here, look at the river and enjoy the different musicians. We have a rota so there's always someone playing. We play all year, but May is the most beautiful month.

I sing folk music because it tells of the troubles people face. Even in a beautiful city like Rome, people have problems. Change is hard here because of the weight of history and there are lots of special interests – the church, the state, the aristocracy. But young people need change.

By Giovanni (aka Johnny) Ursi, folk singer and busker, @johnnyursi

and seasonal, including gourmet open sandwiches, delicate pastas and delectable meat, fish and vegetable mains. (www.facebook.com/pianostrada)

Retrobottega
RISTORANTE €€€

13 MAP P64, C1

Fine dining goes casual at trendy Retrobottega. Here you'll be sitting at a communal table or chatting with the chef during plating at the counter. The creative, multi-course tasting menus aim to elevate ingredients in original ways and are in keeping with the experimental vibe and contemporary decor. (www.retrobottega.com)

La Ciambella
ITALIAN €€

14 MAP P64, D4

This friendly restaurant sits near the Pantheon. Its handsome interior is set over the ruins of the Terme di Agrippa, visible through transparent floor panels, setting an attractive stage for imaginative food. Roman highlights include sweetbreads with wild chicory, chicken and peppers and a delicious *porchetta* (slow-roasted pork) wrap. (www.la-ciambella.it)

Emma
PIZZA €€

15 MAP P64, C6

Offering a contemporary vibe and excellent food, Emma is an all-round winner. Sit on the front terrace or in the airy interior to enjoy excellent antipasti, thin-crust pizzas and classic Roman pasta dishes. The quality of ingredients here is top-notch – think buffalo mozzarella from Paestum, organic tomatoes from the slopes of Vesuvius and Cantabrian anchovies. (www.emmapizzeria.com)

Giulio Passami L'Olio   LAZIO €€

16  MAP P64, A2

This wood-panelled restaurant is full of character. Menu options are chalked up on a board and run the gamut of Roman favourites. The meat platters are excellent, as are the classic *cacio e pepe* and amatriciana pastas. Thin-crust pizzas come topped with tangy mortadella and big dollops of stracciatella cheese, and the pork shank is heroic. It's packed with a lively young crowd in the evening. (www.giuliopassamilolio.it)

Grappolo D'Oro   TRATTORIA €€

17 MAP P64, B5

This busy but welcoming trattoria stands out among the lacklustre options around Campo de' Fiori. Look out for Lazio favourites such as meatballs drenched in intense tomato sauce, pasta with *guanciale* (pork cheek), and rich desserts like *zabaglione* spiked with Marsala wine. During dinner, you may see pasta being hand-rolled at a nearby table. (www.hosteriagrappolodoro.it)

Rimessa Roscioli (p69)

Drinking

L'Angolo Divino　　WINE BAR

18 MAP P64, B6

This warm, timber-ceilinged wine bar is an oasis of calm in the backstreets around Campo de' Fiori. It offers a carefully curated wine list of Italian labels from sommelier Massimo Crippa. There's a good selection of natural and organic wines, platters

Campo de' Fiori

Colourful and busy, **Campo de' Fiori** (Map p64, B5) is a major focus of Roman life: by day it hosts one of the city's best-known **markets**, and its traditional bakery, **Forno Campo de' Fiori** (Map p64, B5; www.fornocampodefiori.com), attracts shoppers from far and wide. By night it transforms into an open-air street party with drinkers spilling out of its bars and restaurants.

For centuries the square was the site of public executions. Philosopher Giordano Bruno was burned for heresy here in 1600 – hence the sinister statue of the hooded monk, created by Ettore Ferrari in 1889. Ironically, the piazza's poetic name (Field of Flowers) is a reference to the open meadow that existed before the square was laid in the mid-15th century.

of regional cheeses and cured meats, and a small daily menu. (www.angolodivino.it)

Il Goccetto　　WINE BAR

19 MAP P64, A4

This authentic *vino e olio* (wine and oil) shop has everything you could want in a wine bar: a woody, bottle-lined interior, a cheerful crowd of locals and first-timers, tasty food (cheese and cured-meat platters €18 for two persons) and a serious 800-strong wine list with plenty of choices by the glass. (www.facebook.com/llgoccetto)

Caffè Sant'Eustachio　　COFFEE

20 MAP P64, C3

Always busy, this small and unassuming historic cafe near the Pantheon serves some of the best coffee in town. Its secret? Baristas beat the first drops of an espresso with several teaspoons of sugar to create a frothy paste to which they add the rest of the coffee. The result is superbly smooth. (https://caffesanteustachio.com)

Roscioli Caffè　　CAFE

21 MAP P64, C6

In Rome, the Roscioli name is a guarantee of good things, and this cafe doesn't disappoint. The coffee is luxurious and the pastries, petits fours and *panini* are artfully crafted. Given its popularity, it's worth booking a seat inside. (www.rosciolicaffe.com)

Caffè Sant'Eustachio

Open Baladin
CRAFT BEER

22 MAP P64, C6

This modern pub near Campo de' Fiori has long been a leading light in Rome's craft-beer scene, and with 40 beers on tap and up to 100 bottled brews (many from Italian artisanal microbreweries), it's a top place for a pint. As well as great beer, expect burgers (€9 to €18), a laid-back vibe and a young, international crowd. (www.openbaladinroma.it)

Il Piccolo
BAR

23 MAP P64, B3

This tiny wine bar on busy Via del Governo Vecchio is easy to miss. But that would mean missing out on a well-loved locale with knowledgeable staff and an intriguing selection of wines by the glass. Plates of *bruschetta*, *salumi* and cheese are also available. It's open until 2am.

La Casa del Caffè Tazza d'Oro
COFFEE

24 MAP P64, D3

A busy cafe with burnished 1940s fittings, this is one of Rome's most characterful coffee houses. Its position near the Pantheon makes it touristy but its coffees are brilliant – the espresso hits the mark every time and there's also a range of delicious *caffè* concoctions, including *granita di caffè*, a crushed-ice coffee served with whipped cream. (www. tazzadorocoffeeshop.com)

Entertainment

Teatro Argentina · THEATRE

25 ⭐ MAP P64, D5

Founded in 1732, Rome's top theatre is one of three managed by the Teatro di Roma, along with the **Teatro India** (www.teatrodiroma.net) and Teatro di Villa Torlonia. Rossini's *Barber of Seville* premiered here in 1816, and these days it stages a wide-ranging programme of classic and contemporary drama (mostly in Italian),

Speakeasy Cocktails

The *centro storico* has some serious speakeasy bars. The only problem is finding them. The most notorious is **Jerry Thomas Project** (www.thejerrythomasproject.it), a Prohibition era–inspired speakeasy that has been listed five times in the World's 50 Best Bars. But you'll need to figure out the password to gain entry. Likewise, **Club Derrière** (Map p64, D2; www.facebook.com/clubderriereroma) is buried in the back room of a trattoria (Osteria delle Coppelle).

Other popular spots include **Argot** (Map p64, A4) with a vintage vibe (there's no sign, just ring the bell) and buzzy **Bar del Fico** (Map p64, B3; www.bardelfico.com).

Shopping

Confetteria Moriondo & Gariglio · CHOCOLATE

26 🔒 MAP P64, E4

Roman poet Trilussa was so smitten with this chocolate shop – established by the Torinese confectioners to the royal house of Savoy – that he was moved to mention it in verse. And we agree: it's a gem. Decorated like an elegant tearoom, it specialises in handmade chocolates and confections such as marrons glacés, many prepared according to original 19th-century recipes.

Co.Ro Jewels · JEWELRY

27 🔒 MAP P64, C2

Fronted by entrepreneurs and jewellers Costanza de Cecco e Giulia Giannini, Co.Ro draws its inspiration from the architecture of the Eternal City. Handcrafted baubles fashioned in gold, sterling silver, bronze and ruthenium recall the arch of the Pantheon, sprawling aqueducts, Borromini's baroque domes and more. (www.corojewels.com)

Chez Dede · CONCEPT STORE

28 🔒 MAP P64, A5

This chic boutique offers a curated selection of both vintage and contemporary designer accessories, fashions, homewares and books. Its signature canvas and leather tote bags are bestsellers, but the original artworks, hand-painted ceramics and limited edition perfumes are lovely, too. (www.chezdede.com)

LUCAMATO/GETTY IMAGES ©

Teatro Argentina

Camiceria Bracci CLOTHING

29 🔒 MAP P64, D2

For most people, a made-to-measure shirt or suit is a luxury beyond their budget, but that's not so in Rome, where tailors still run up elegant outfits at very reasonable prices. Bracci is just such a place and can turn out a quality piece of clothing from a huge array of excellent fabrics in just two days. A shirt costs €58 and a suit €490. (www.braccicamiceriasartoria.com)

Del Giudice FASHION & ACCESSORIES

30 🔒 MAP P64, D2

Established in Rome in 1959, this business produces leather bags, briefcases, wallets, belts and backpacks in its Roman workshop and sells them in this elegant boutique. Remarkably well-priced considering their quality. Purchase off the shelf or have something custom-made. (www.delgiudiceroma.com)

Marta Ray SHOES

31 🔒 MAP P64, A2

Women's ballet flats and elegant, everyday bags in rainbow colours and super-soft leather are the hallmarks of the Rome-born Marta Ray brand. At this store, one of three in town, you'll find a selection of trademark flats as well as ankle boots and an attractive line in modern, beautifully designed handbags. (www.martaray.it)

Explore ⊛

Vatican City, Borgo & Prati

The Vatican, the world's smallest state, sits over the river from Rome's historic centre. Centred on St Peter's Basilica, it boasts some of Italy's most revered artworks, many housed in the vast Vatican Museums. Bookended by St Peter's and the hulking Castel Sant'Angelo is the quaint Borgo Pio district, while beyond are the stylish eateries and boutiques of Prati.

The Short List

○ **Sistine Chapel (p78)** *Gazing heavenwards at Michelangelo's ceiling frescoes and his terrifying Last Judgment.*

○ **St Peter's Basilica (p84)** *Being blown away by the supersized opulence of the Vatican's showpiece church.*

○ **Castel Sant'Angelo (p92)** *Revelling in wonderful rooftop views from this landmark castle.*

○ **Stanze di Raffaello (p78)** *Marvelling at Raphael's masterpiece, La Scuola di Atene, in the Vatican Museums.*

Getting There & Around

🚌 From Termini, bus 40 is the quickest one to the Vatican: bus 64 runs a similar route but stops more often. Bus 81 runs to Piazza del Risorgimento via the centro storico (historic centre).

Ⓜ Take line A to Ottaviano-San Pietro.

🚊 Tram 19 serves Piazza del Risorgimento via San Lorenzo and Villa Borghese.

Neighbourhood Map on p90

St Peter's Basilica MISTERVLAD/SHUTTERSTOCK ©

Top Experience

Admire Masterpieces in the Vatican Museums

◉ MAP P90, C3

www.museivaticani.va

Visiting the Vatican Museums is an unforgettable experience. With some 7km of exhibitions and more masterpieces than many small countries can call their own, this vast museum complex boasts one of the world's greatest art collections. Highlights include classical statuary in the Museo Pio-Clementino, a suite of rooms frescoed by Raphael, and the Michelangelo-decorated Sistine Chapel.

Pinacoteca

Often overlooked by visitors, the papal picture gallery displays paintings dating from the 11th to 19th centuries, with works by Giotto, Fra' Angelico, Filippo Lippi, Perugino, Titian, Guido Reni, Guercino, Pietro da Cortona, Caravaggio and Leonardo da Vinci.

Look out for a trio of paintings by Raphael in Room VIII – the *Madonna di Foligno* (Madonna of Folignano), the *Incoronazione della Vergine* (Crowning of the Virgin), and *La Trasfigurazione* (Transfiguration), which was completed by his students after his death in 1520. Other highlights include Leonardo da Vinci's haunting and unfinished *San Gerolamo* (St Jerome), and Caravaggio's *Deposizione* (Deposition from the Cross).

Museo Chiaramonti & Braccio Nuovo

This museum is effectively the long corridor that runs down the lower east side of the Palazzetto di Belvedere. Its walls are lined with thousands of statues and busts representing everything from immortal gods to playful cherubs and ugly Roman patricians.

Near the end of the hall, off to the right, is the Braccio Nuovo (New Wing), which contains a celebrated statue of the Nile as a reclining god covered by 16 babies.

Museo Pio-Clementino

This stunning museum contains some of the Vatican's finest classical statuary, including the peerless *Apollo Belvedere* and the 1st-century BCE *Laocoön,* both in the **Cortile Ottagono** (Octagonal Courtyard).

Before you go into the courtyard, take a moment to admire the 1st-century *Apoxyomenos*, one of the earliest known sculptures to depict a figure with a raised arm.

★ **Top Tips**

○ Avoid horrendous queues: book tickets (€4 fee) online.

○ Last Sunday of the month the museums are free (and busy).

○ Consider an audioguide (adult/child €8/6) or *Guide to the Vatican Museums and City* (€13).

○ Tuesdays and Thursdays are quietest; Wednesday mornings are good; late afternoons are better; avoid Mondays and rainy days.

○ Check the website for excellent tours or book a tour with **The Roman Guy** or **Understanding Rome**.

○ Strollers are permitted.

✗ **Take a Break**

There's a bistro in the Cortile della Pigna, self-service cafeterias and a cafe near the Pinacoteca.

For a bite, head to Bonci Pizzarium (p92), one of Rome's best sliced pizza joints.

To the left as you enter the courtyard, the *Apollo Belvedere* is a 2nd-century Roman copy of a 4th-century-BCE Greek bronze. A beautifully proportioned representation of the sun god Apollo, it's considered one of the great masterpieces of classical sculpture. Nearby, the *Laocoön* depicts the mythical death of the Trojan priest who warned his fellow citizens not to take the wooden horse left by the Greeks.

Back inside, the **Sala degli Animali** is filled with sculpted creatures and magnificent 4th-century mosaics. Continuing on, you come to the **Sala delle Muse** (Room of the Muses), centred on the *Torso Belvedere,* another of the museum's must-sees. A fragment of a muscular 1st-century-BCE Greek sculpture, this was found in Campo de' Fiori and used by Michelangelo as a model for his *ignudi* (male nudes) in the Sistine Chapel.

The next room, the **Sala Rotonda** (Round Room), contains a number of colossal statues, including a gilded-bronze *Ercole* (Hercules) and an exquisite floor mosaic. The enormous basin in the centre of the room was found at Nero's Domus Aurea and is made out of a single piece of red porphyry stone.

Museo Gregoriano Egizio

Founded by Pope Gregory XVI in 1839, this Egyptian museum displays pieces taken from Egypt in ancient Roman times.

Sala Rotonda

Museo Gregoriano Etrusco

At the top of the 18th-century Simonetti staircase, this fascinating museum contains artefacts unearthed in the Etruscan tombs of northern Lazio, as well as a superb collection of vases and Roman antiquities.

Galleria dei Candelabri & Galleria degli Arazzi

The **Galleria dei Candelabri** is packed with classical sculpture and several elegantly carved candelabras that give the gallery its name. The corridor continues through to the **Galleria degli Arazzi** (Tapestry Gallery) and its huge hanging tapestries.

Galleria delle Carte Geografiche & Sala Sobieski

One of the unsung heroes of the Vatican Museums, the 120m-long Map Gallery is hung with 40 huge topographical maps. These were created between 1580 and 1583 for Pope Gregory XIII based on drafts by Ignazio Danti, one of the leading cartographers of his day.

Beyond the gallery, the **Sala Sobieski** is named after an enormous 19th-century painting depicting the victory of the Polish King John III Sobieski over the Turks in 1683.

Stanze di Raffaello

These four frescoed chambers, currently undergoing partial restoration, were part of Pope Julius II's private apartments. Raphael himself painted the Stanza della Segnatura (1508–11) and Stanza d'Eliodoro (1512–14), while the Stanza dell'Incendio (1514–17) and Sala di Costantino (1517–24) were decorated by students following his designs.

The first room you come to is the **Sala di Costantino**, which features a huge fresco depicting Constantine's defeat of Maxentius at the battle of Milvian Bridge.

The **Stanza d'Eliodoro**, which was used for private audiences, takes its name from the *Cacciata d'Eliodoro* (Expulsion of Heliodorus from the Temple), an allegorical work reflecting Pope Julius II's policy of forcing foreign powers off Church lands. To its right, the *Messa di Bolsena* (Mass of Bolsena) shows Julius paying homage to the relic of a 13th-century miracle at the lakeside town of Bolsena. Next is the *Incontro di Leone Magno con Attila* (Encounter of Leo the Great with Attila) by Raphael and his school and, on the fourth wall, the *Liberazione di San Pietro* (Liberation of St Peter), a brilliant work illustrating Raphael's masterful ability to depict light.

The **Stanza della Segnatura**, Julius' study and library, was the first room that Raphael painted, and it's here that you'll find his great masterpiece, *La Scuola di Atene* (The School of Athens), featuring philosophers and scholars gathered around Plato and Aristotle. The seated figure in front of the steps is believed to be Michelangelo, while the figure of Plato is said to be a portrait of Leonardo da Vinci, and Euclide (the bald man bending over) is Bramante. Raphael also included a self-portrait in the lower right corner – he's the second figure from the right.

The most famous work in the **Stanza dell'Incendio di Borgo** is the *Incendio di Borgo* (Fire in the Borgo), which depicts Pope Leo IV extinguishing a fire by making the sign of the cross. The ceiling was painted by Raphael's master, Perugino.

Sistine Chapel

The jewel in the Vatican crown, the Cappella Sistina (Sistine Chapel) is home to two of the world's most famous works of art – Michelangelo's ceiling frescoes (1508–12) and his *Giudizio Universale* (Last Judgment; 1536–41). The chapel also serves an important religious function as the place where the conclave meets to elect a new pope.

Ceiling Frescoes

The Sistine Chapel provided the greatest challenge of Michelangelo's career and painting the entire 800-sq-m ceiling at a height of more than 20m pushed him to the limits of his genius.

The focus of his design, which is best viewed from the chapel's main entrance in the east wall, are nine central panels depicting stories from the book of Genesis. Set around these are 20 athletic male nudes known as *ignudi* and a colourful cast of sibyls, prophets and biblical figures.

As you look up from the east wall, the first panel is the *Drunkenness of Noah*, followed by *The Flood*, and the *Sacrifice of Noah*. Next, *Original Sin and Banishment from the Garden of Eden* famously depicts Adam and Eve being sent packing after accepting the forbidden fruit from Satan, represented by a snake with the body of a woman coiled around a tree. The *Creation of Eve* is then followed by the *Creation of Adam*. This, one of the most famous images in Western art, shows a bearded God pointing his finger at Adam, thus bringing him to life. Completing the sequence are the *Separation of Land from Sea*; the *Creation of the Sun, Moon and Plants*; and the *Separation of Light from Darkness*, featuring a fearsome God reaching out to touch the sun.

Giudizio Universale

Michelangelo's second stint in the Sistine Chapel resulted in the *Last Judgment*, his highly charged depiction of Christ's second coming on the 200-sq-m western wall.

It shows Christ – in the centre near the top – passing sentence over the souls of the dead as they are torn from their graves to face him. The saved get to stay up in heaven (in the upper right); the damned are sent down to face the demons in hell (in the bottom right).

Vatican Museums

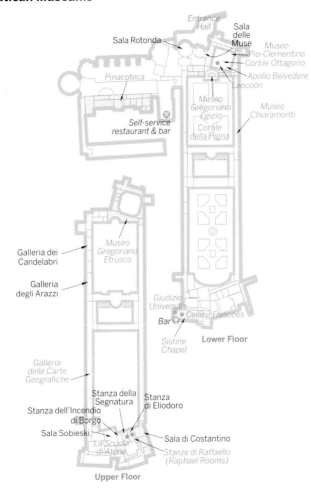

Entrance Hall

Sala Rotonda

Sala delle Muse

Museo Pio-Clementino

Cortile Ottagono

Apollo Belvedere

Laocoön

Pinacoteca

Self-service restaurant & bar

Museo Gregoriano Egizio

Cortile della Pigna

Museo Chiaramonti

Galleria dei Candelabri

Museo Gregoriano Etrusco

Galleria degli Arazzi

Giudizio Universale

Bar

Ceiling Frescoes

Sistine Chapel

Lower Floor

Galleria delle Carte Geografiche

Stanza della Segnatura

Stanza di Eliodoro

Stanza dell'Incendio di Borgo

Sala Sobieski

Sala di Costantino

La Scuola di Atene

Stanze di Raffaello (Raphael Rooms)

Upper Floor

Top Experience 📷
Ponder Epic Power at St Peter's Basilica

◉ MAP P90, C5
www.vatican.va

In a city of outstanding churches, none can hold a candle to St Peter's, Italy's largest, richest and most spectacular basilica. A monument to centuries of artistic genius, it boasts many spectacular works of art, including three of Italy's most celebrated masterpieces: Michelangelo's Pietà, his soaring dome and Bernini's 29m-high bronze baldachin (canopy) over the papal altar.

St Peter's Square

Laid out in front of the basilica, the Vatican's epic central piazza was created between 1656 and 1667 to a design by Gian Lorenzo Bernini. Seen from above, it resembles a giant keyhole with two semicircular colonnades of Doric columns, encircling a giant ellipse that straightens out to funnel believers into the basilica. The effect was deliberate – Bernini described the colonnades as representing 'the motherly arms of the church'.

The Facade

Built between 1608 and 1612, Maderno's immense facade is 48m high and 115m wide. Eight 27m-high columns support the upper attic on which 13 statues stand representing Christ the Redeemer, St John the Baptist and the 11 apostles. The central balcony is known as the **Loggia della Benedizione**, and it's from here that the pope delivers his *Urbi et Orbi* blessing at Christmas and Easter.

In the grand atrium, the **Porta Santa** (Holy Door) is opened only in Jubilee years.

Interior – The Nave

Dominating the centre of the basilica is Bernini's 29m-high **baldachin**. Supported by four spiral columns and made with bronze taken from the Pantheon, it stands over the **papal altar**, also known as the Altar of the Confession. In front, Carlo Maderno's **Confessione** stands over the site where St Peter was originally buried.

Above the baldachin, Michelangelo's **dome** soars to a height of 119m. Based on Brunelleschi's design for the Duomo in Florence, it's supported by four massive stone **piers**, each named after the saint whose statue adorns its Bernini-designed niche. The saints are all associated with the basilica's four major relics: the lance **St Longinus** supposedly used

★ Top Tips

○ Dress appropriately if you want to get in – no shorts, miniskirts or bare shoulders.

○ Free, two-hour English-language tours are run by seminarians from the Pontifical North American College (www.pnac. org). These start at 2.15pm every weekday at the statue of St Peter on the south side of the piazza. No tickets necessary, but check the website for dates.

○ Queues are inevitable at the security checks, but they move quickly.

○ Lines are generally shorter during lunch hours and late afternoon.

✕ Take a Break

For a light lunch, head to the picturesque pedestrian street of Borgo Pio, which is lined with casual eateries with lovely outdoor seating. Or, for something more memorable, join the serious foodies at Il Sorpasso (p92).

to pierce Christ's side; the cloth with which **St Veronica** was said to have wiped Jesus' face; a fragment of the Cross collected by **St Helena**; and the head of **St Andrew**.

At the base of the **Pier of St Longinus** is Arnolfo di Cambio's much-loved 13th-century bronze **statue of St Peter**, whose right foot has been worn down by centuries of caresses.

Behind the altar, the tribune is home to Bernini's extraordinary **Cattedra di San Pietro**. A vast gilded bronze throne held aloft by four 5m-high saints, it's centred on a wooden seat that was once thought to have been St Peter's but in fact dates from the 9th century. Above, light shines through a yellow window framed by a gilded mass of golden angels and adorned with a dove to represent the Holy Spirit.

To the right of the throne, Bernini's **monument to Urban VIII** depicts the pope flanked by the figures of Charity and Justice.

Interior – Left Aisle

In the roped-off left transept, the **Cappella della Madonna della Colonna** takes its name from the Madonna that stares out from Giacomo della Porta's marble altar. To its right, above the **tomb of St Leo the Great**, is a fine relief by Alessandro Algardi. Under the next arch is Bernini's last work in the basilica, the **monument to Alexander VII**.

Halfway down the left aisle, the **Cappella Clementina** is named

Interior of St Peter's Basilica

History of the Basilica

The original St Peter's – which lies beneath the current basilica – was commissioned by the Emperor Constantine and built around 349 on the site where St Peter is said to have been buried between 64 and 67 CE. But like many medieval churches, it eventually fell into disrepair and it wasn't until the mid-15th century that efforts were made to restore it, first by Pope Nicholas V and then, rather more successfully, by Julius II.

In 1506 construction began on Bramante's design for a new basilica based on a Greek-cross plan. But on Bramante's death in 1514, building ground to a halt as architects, including Raphael and Antonio da Sangallo, tried to modify his original plans. Little progress was made and it wasn't until Michelangelo took over in 1547 at the age of 72 that the situation changed. Michelangelo simplified Bramante's plans and drew up designs for what was to become his greatest architectural achievement, the dome. He never lived to see the cupola built, though, and it was left to Giacomo della Porta and Domenico Fontana to finish it in 1590.

With the dome in place, Carlo Maderno inherited the project in 1605. He designed the monumental facade and lengthened the nave towards the piazza.

The basilica was finally consecrated in 1626.

after Clement VIII, who had Giacomo della Porta decorate it for the Jubilee of 1600. Beneath the altar is the **tomb of St Gregory the Great** and, to the left, a **monument to Pope Pius VII** by Thorvaldsen.

The next arch shelters Alessandro Algardi's 16th-century **monument to Leo XI**. Beyond it, the richly decorated **Cappella del Coro** was created by Giovanni Battista Ricci to designs by Giacomo della Porta. The **monument to Innocent VIII** by Antonio Pollaiuolo in the next aisle arch is a recreation of a monument from the old basilica.

Continuing on, the **Cappella della Presentazione** contains two of St Peter's most modern works: a black relief **monument to John XXIII** by Emilio Greco, and a **monument to Benedict XV** by Pietro Canonica.

Under the next arch are the so-called **Stuart monuments**. On the right is the monument to Clementina Sobieska, wife of James Stuart, by Filippo Barigioni, and on the left is Canova's vaguely erotic monument to the last three members of the Stuart clan, the pretenders to the English throne who died in exile in Rome.

Interior – Right Aisle

At the head of the right aisle is Michelangelo's hauntingly beautiful **Pietà**. Sculpted when he was only 25 (in 1499), it's the only work the artist ever signed – his signature is etched into the sash across the Madonna's breast.

Nearby, a **red floor disc** marks the spot where Charlemagne and later Holy Roman emperors were crowned by the pope.

On a pillar just beyond *Pietà*, Carlo Fontana's gilt and bronze **monument to Queen Christina of Sweden** commemorates the far-from-holy Swedish monarch who converted to Catholicism in 1655.

Moving on, you'll come to the **Cappella di San Sebastiano**, home of Pope John Paul II's tomb, and the **Cappella del Santissimo Sacramento**, a sumptuously decorated baroque chapel with works by Borromini, Bernini and Pietro da Cortona.

Beyond the chapel, the grandiose **monument to Gregory XIII** sits near the roped-off **Cappella Gregoriana**, a chapel built by Gregory XIII from designs by Michelangelo.

Much of the right transept is closed off, but you can still make out the **monument to Clement XIII**, one of Canova's most famous works.

Pietà by Michelangelo

Dome

From the **dome** entrance on the right of the basilica's main portico, you can walk the 551 steps to the top or take a small lift halfway and then follow on foot for the last 320 steps. Either way, it's a long, steep climb. But make it to the top, and you're rewarded with stunning views from a perch 120m above St Peter's Square. If you suffer from vertigo or claustrophobia, the trip to the top isn't recommended.

Museo Storico Artistico

Accessed from the left nave, the **Museo Storico Artistico** sparkles with sacred relics. Highlights include a tabernacle by Donatello; the *Colonna Santa*, a 4th-century Byzantine column from the earlier church; and the 6th-century *Crux Vaticana* (Vatican Cross), a jewel-encrusted crucifix presented by the emperor Justinian II to the original basilica.

Vatican Grottoes

Extending beneath the basilica, the **Vatican Grottoes** contain the tombs and sarcophagi of numerous popes, as well as several columns from the original 4th-century basilica. The entrance is in the Pier of St Andrew.

Papal Audiences

Papal audiences are held at 10am on Wednesdays, usually in St Peter's Square but sometimes in the nearby Aula delle Udienze Pontificie Paolo VI (Paul VI Audience Hall). You'll need to book free tickets in advance. No tickets are required for the pope's Sunday blessing, at noon in St Peter's Square. See the Vatican website (www.vatican.va/various/prefettura/index_en.html) for more details.

Tomb of St Peter

Excavations beneath the basilica have uncovered part of the original church and what archaeologists believe is the **Tomb of St Peter** (www.scavi.va). In 1942, the bones of an elderly, strongly built man were found in a box hidden behind a wall covered by pilgrims' graffiti. And while the Vatican has never definitively claimed that the bones belong to St Peter, in 1968 Pope Paul VI said that they had been identified in a way that the Vatican considered 'convincing'.

The excavations can only be visited by guided tour. For further details, and to book a tour (this must be done well in advance), check out the website of the **Ufficio Scavi** (Excavations Office; www.scavi.va). Minimum age for admission is 15 years old.

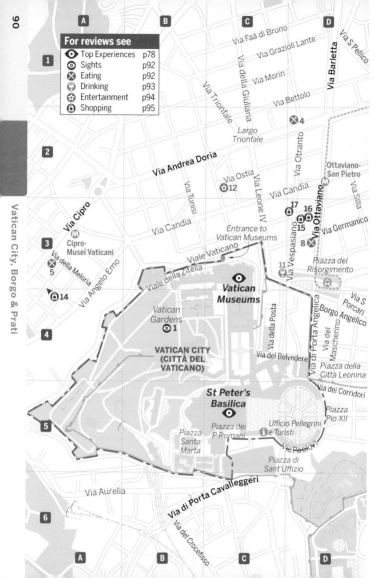

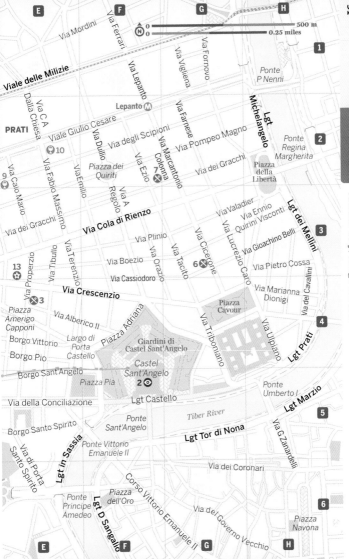

Via Mordini
Via Ferrari
Viale delle Milizie
Via Lepanto
Via Vigliena
Via Fornovo
Ponte P Nenni
Lgt Michelangelo

Via C A Dalla Chiesa
PRATI
Viale Giulio Cesare
Lepanto Ⓜ
Via degli Scipioni
Via Duilio
Via Ezio
Via Farnese
Via Marcantonio Colonna
Via Pompeo Magno
Via dei Gracchi
Ponte Regina Margherita
Piazza della Libertà

Via Caio Mario
Via Fabio Massimo
Via Emilio
Via A Regolo
Piazza dei Quiriti
7 ❌
Via Valadier
Via Ennio Quirini Visconti
Lgt dei Mellini

Via dei Gracchi
Via Cola di Rienzo
Via Plinio
Via Cicerone
Via Lucrezio Caro
Via Gioachino Belli
Via Pietro Cossa

Via Tibullo
Via Terenzio
Via Boezio
Via Orazio
Via Tacito
6 ❌
Via Marianna Dionigi
Via del Cavallini

13 ⭐
Via Properzio
Via Crescenzio
Via Cassiodoro
Piazza Cavour
Lgt Prati

❌3
Piazza Amerigo Capponi
Via Alberico II
Piazza Adriana
Via Triboniano
Via Ulpiano

Borgo Vittorio
Largo di Porta Castello
Giardini di Castel Sant'Angelo
Ponte Umberto I
Lgt Marzio

Borgo Pio
Borgo Sant'Angelo
Castel Sant'Angelo
2 ◎
Via G Zanardelli

Piazza Pia
Lgt Castello
Tiber River

Via della Conciliazione
Ponte Sant'Angelo
Lgt Tor di Nona

Borgo Santo Spirito
Lgt in Sassia
Via di Porta Santo Spirito
Ponte Vittorio Emanuele II
Via dei Coronari

Ponte Principe Amedeo
Lgt D Sangallo
Piazza dell'Oro
Corso Vittorio Emanuele II
Via del Governo Vecchio
Piazza Navona

9 🚌
10 🚌

Sights

Vatican Gardens

GARDENS

1 ◉ MAP P90, B4

Up to a third of the Vatican is covered by the perfectly manicured Vatican Gardens, which contain fortifications, grottoes, monuments, fountains and the state's tiny heliport and train station. Visits are by guided tour only – either on foot (two hours) or by open-air bus (45 minutes) – for which you'll need to book at least a week in advance. (www.museivaticani.va)

Castel Sant'Angelo

MUSEUM, CASTLE

2 ◉ MAP P90, F5

With its chunky round keep, this castle is an instantly recognisable landmark. Built as a mausoleum for the emperor Hadrian, it was converted into a papal fortress in the 6th century and named after an angelic vision that Pope Gregory the Great had in 590. Nowadays, it is a moody and dramatic keep that houses the **Museo Nazionale di Castel Sant'Angelo** and its grand collection of paintings, sculpture, military memorabilia and medieval firearms. (www.castelsantangelo.beniculturali.it)

Eating

Il Sorpasso

ITALIAN €€

3 ✕ MAP P90, E4

This Prati hotspot with outdoor seating and a cool paired-back

look turns out sensational food. The menu changes daily and features small plates of aged prosciutto topped by sweet green figs, salads of bitter chicory doused in a salty anchovy sauce and homemade pastas with rabbit from Viterbo and slow roast pork with roasted radicchio and Jerusalem artichokes. (www.sorpasso.info)

Trattoria Gallo Brillo

LAZIO €€

4 ✕ MAP P90, D2

Authentic Gallo Brillo has a vintage, wood-panelled dining room and simple tables crammed with hungry diners, who come for thoroughly Roman fare. Highlights include *stringozzi allo stracotto* (pasta with a rich stew sauce), pasta with mussels and green tomatoes, rabbit sautéed with herbs, glazed ribs and more. The sour cherry tart with a glass of grappa is a great finish. (www.facebook.com/gallobrilloroma)

Bonci Pizzarium

PIZZA €

5 ✕ MAP P90, A3

Gabriele Bonci's acclaimed *pizzeria a taglio* serves Rome's best pizza by the slice, bar none. Scissor-cut squares of soft, springy base are topped with original combinations of seasonal ingredients and served for immediate consumption. There are only a couple of benches and stools for the hungry hordes. (www.bonci.it)

L'Arcangelo

RISTORANTE €€€

6 MAP P90, G3

Styled as an informal bistro with wood panelling, leather banquettes and casual table settings, L'Arcangelo enjoys a stellar local reputation. Dishes are modern and creative yet still undeniably Roman in their execution, with an emphasis on seasonal ingredients. A further plus is a well-curated wine list. (www.larcangelo.com)

Gelateria dei Gracchi

GELATO €

7 MAP P90, F2

This is the original location of a small and highly regarded local chain of artisanal *gelaterie*. The proprietors here only use fresh fruit in season, so flavours vary. What stays constant is the quality of the icy delights. (www.gelateriadeigracchi.it)

Fa-Bìo

VEGETARIAN €

8 MAP P90, D3

Sandwiches, wraps, salads, breakfast bowls, soup and fresh juices are all prepared with speed, skill and fresh locally sourced organic ingredients at this busy place, which is vegan and vegetarian friendly. Great for a quick lunchtime bite to eat in or take away.

Drinking

Del Frate

WINE BAR

9 MAP P90, E2

Locals love this upmarket *enoteca* (wine bar) with its simple wooden tables, bottle-lined walls and high-

Castel Sant'Angelo

SYLVAIN SONNET/SHUTTERSTOCK ©

Local Favourites

Museo dell'Arte Salvata

(Octagonal Hall; Map p90; www.museonazionaleromano. beniculturali.it/museoartesalvata) Housed in the Aula Ottagona (an old planetarium), this museum displays stolen ancient artefacts recovered by the police. The pieces and place are very beautiful.

Parco degli Acquedotti

This park is one of Rome's most overlooked. Walking there is like going back in time, stepping back from the surrounding chaos into the meadows and trees among the naturally stunning ruins and magnificent Roman acqueducts.

Monti Neighbourhood

We like to go for Sunday walks in Monti among the art shops, fashion studios and workshops. We always have a *cornetto e cappuccino* in one of the two bars in Piazza della Madonna dei Monti. Then we visit the Mercato Monti and walk up Via Baccina to the end for a beautiful view over the Fori Imperiali.

By Marco & Serena Gigli, artisan jewellers, @giglilab

ceilinged brick-arched rooms. The extensive wine list is complemented with a selection of platters including a formidable cheese selection (from Sicilian ricotta to Piedmontese *robiola*). (www.enotecadelfrate.it)

Sciascia Caffè

CAFE

10   MAP P90, E2

There are several contenders for the best coffee in town, and the *caffè eccellente* served at this polished old-school cafe in Prati, which opened in 1919, is most definitely one of them. The house speciality is velvety smooth espresso served in a delicate cup lined with melted chocolate. (http://sciasciacaffe1919.it)

Be.re

CRAFT BEER

11   MAP P90, C3

With its high vaulted ceilings and narrow pavement tables, this is a good spot for Italian craft beers – there are 23 on tap. And should hunger strike, there's a branch of hit takeaway Trapizzino right next door that offers table service at Be.re. (www.facebook.com/berebirreriaroma)

Entertainment

Alexanderplatz

JAZZ

12   MAP P90, C2

Intimate, underground and hard to find – look for the discreet black door near the corner – Rome's most celebrated jazz club draws top Italian and international performers and a respectful cosmopolitan crowd. Book a table for the best stage views or to dine here. Performances begin at 9.30pm. (www.alexanderplatzjazz.com)

Fonclea Pub LIVE MUSIC

13 ⭐ MAP P90, E3

Fonclea is a great little pub venue, with nightly gigs by bands playing everything from jazz and soul to pop, rock and doo-wop. Get in the mood with a drink during the daily happy hour (6pm to 8.30pm). There are several cocktail bars nearby with outdoor tables. (www.fonclea.it)

Shopping

Paciotti FOOD & DRINKS

14 🅐 MAP P90, A4

This family-run deli is a fantasyland of Italian edibles. Whole prosciutto hams hang in profusion. Cheeses, olive oil, dried pasta, balsamic vinegar, wine and truffle pâtés crowd the shelves, and can be bubble-wrapped and vacuum-sealed for travel. (www.facebook. com/paciottisalumeria)

Orafo Gigli JEWELLERY

15 🅐 MAP P90, D3

Seventh-generation Roman, Marco and his wife Serena come from a family of goldsmiths and gem-cutters. As a result, they have an eye for interesting stones, which they refashion into pieces inspired by ancient Roman designs. The coin rings (€70) make stunning souvenirs, but take some time in this tiny shop and you'll see antique Sicilian coral strings, rock crystal necklaces embellished with gold and strands of semi-precious stones in iridescent colours.

Antica Manifattura Cappelli HATS

16 🅐 MAP P90, D3

A throwback to a more elegant age, the 1930s atelier-boutique of milliner Patrizia Fabri turns out beautifully crafted hats. Choose from the off-the-peg line of straw Panamas, vintage cloches, felt berets and tweed deerstalkers, or have one made to measure. Prices range from about €70 to €300. (www.antica-cappelleria.it)

Brugnoli CONCEPT STORE

17 🅐 MAP P90, D3

For smart footwear from heritage Roman and international brands, nip into this cool shop-come-lounge in Prati. The shoes here are superbly made and sit beside a well-curated selection of clothes and accessories. (https:// brugnolishop.bigcartel.com)

Explore ◈
Tridente, Trevi & the Quirinale

Counting the Trevi Fountain and Spanish Steps among its A-list sights, this part of Rome is debonair and touristy. Designer boutiques, fashionable bars and historic cafes crowd the streets of Tridente, while the area around Piazza Barberini and the Trevi Fountain, within shouting distance of the presidential Quirinale palace, harbours multiple art galleries and eateries.

The Short List

○ **Spanish Steps (p100)** *People-watching and selfie-snapping while climbing this city icon.*

○ **Basilica di Santa Maria del Popolo (p104)** *Marvelling at Caravaggio's two masterworks in the Cerasi Chapel.*

○ **Villa Medici (p104)** *Touring this Renaissance villa with its formal gardens and wonderful city views.*

○ **Gallerie Nazionali: Palazzo Barberini (p104)** *Admiring works by Raphael, Caravaggio, El Greco and Pietro da Cortona in a palace built for a pope.*

○ **Shopping (p111)** *Browsing designer fashions, artisanal perfumes, silverware, and much more besides, on and around Via dei Condotti.*

Getting There & Around

Ⓜ Barberini for the Trevi and Quirinale areas; Spagna and Flaminio for Tridente. All three stations are on line A.

🚌 Numerous buses serve Piazza Barberini; many stop at the southern end of Via del Corso and on Via del Tritone for Tridente.

Neighbourhood Map on p102

Piazza del Popolo VLADIMIR SAZONOV/SHUTTERSTOCK ©

Top Experience
Toss a Coin in the Trevi Fountain

Rome's most famous fountain, the iconic Fontana di Trevi, is a baroque extravaganza – a foaming white-marble masterpiece with a basin of emerald water that almost fills an entire piazza. The flamboyant ensemble, 20m wide and 26m high, was designed by Nicola Salvi in 1732 and depicts the chariot of the sea-god Oceanus being led by Tritons accompanied by seahorses that represent the moods of the sea.

◉ MAP P102, D6

Aqua Virgo

The fountain depicts the sea-god Oceanus in a shell-shaped chariot being led by Tritons with seahorses – one wild, one docile – rearing above the cascading water. The water comes from the Aqua Virgo, an underground aqueduct that is over 2000 years old. It was built by General Agrippa under Augustus and brings water from the Salone springs around 19km away. The *tre vie* (three roads) that converge at the fountain give it its name.

Salvi's Urn

To the eastern side of the fountain is a large round stone urn. The story goes that during the fountain's construction, Salvi was harassed by a barber, who had a nearby shop and was critical of the work in progress. Thus the sculptor added this urn in order to block the irritating critic.

Coin Tossing

The famous tradition (inaugurated in the 1954 film *Three Coins in the Fountain*) is to toss a coin into the fountain, thus ensuring your return to Rome. An estimated €3000 is thrown into the Trevi each day. This money is collected daily and goes to the Catholic charity Caritas, with its yield increasing significantly since the crackdown on people extracting the money for themselves.

Trevi on Camera

Most famously, Trevi Fountain is where movie star Anita Ekberg cavorted in Federico Fellini's classic *La Dolce Vita* (1960); apparently she wore waders under her iconic black dress but still shivered during the winter shoot.

In 2016, fashion house Fendi staged a show at the fountain following its €2.18 million sponsorship of the fountain's restoration.

★ **Top Tips**

○ Coin-tossing etiquette: throw with your right hand, over your left shoulder with your back facing the fountain.

○ Paddling or bathing in the fountain is strictly forbidden, as is eating and drinking on the steps leading down to the water. Both crimes risk an on-the-spot fine of up to €450.

○ The fountain gets very busy during the day; visit later in the evening when it's beautifully lit instead.

✕ **Take a Break**

Recommended dining choices near the fountain include lovely Piccolo Arancio (p106), turning out contemporary Roman classics and bustling Pane e Salami (p107) for top-notch sandwiches.

Top Experience 📷

Watch the Sunset at the Spanish Steps

⊙ MAP P102, C4

Forming a picture-perfect backdrop to Piazza di Spagna, this statement sweep of stairs is one of the city's major icons and public meeting points. Though officially named the Scalinata della Trinità dei Monti, the stairs are popularly called the Spanish Steps. It's a perfect people-watching perch with one of the best city views from its summit.

Spanish Steps

Piazza di Spagna was named after the Spanish Embassy to the Holy See, but the staircase – 135 gleaming steps designed by the Italian Francesco de Sanctis – was built in 1725 with a legacy from the French. The dazzling stairs reopened in September 2016 after a €1.5 million clean-up job funded by jewellers Bulgari.

Chiesa della Trinità dei Monti

This landmark **church** (Map p102; http://trinitadeimonti.net/it/chiesa) was commissioned by Louis XII of France and consecrated in 1585. Apart from great city views from its front steps, it's notable for its wonderful frescoes by Daniele da Volterra.

Keats-Shelley House

Overlooking the steps, this **house-museum** (www.keats-shelley-house.org) is where Romantic poet John Keats died in February 1821. Keats came to Rome in 1820 to try to improve his health, and rented two rooms with a painter companion, Joseph Severn (1793–1879).

Fontana della Barcaccia

At the foot of the steps, the fountain of a sinking boat, the **Barcaccia** (1627), is believed to be by Pietro Bernini, father of the more famous Gian Lorenzo. The sunken design is a clever piece of engineering to compensate for low water pressure – it's fed by an ancient Roman aqueduct, the Aqua Virgo.

Colonna dell'Immacolata

To the southeast of the piazza, adjacent Piazza Mignanelli is dominated by the Colonna dell'Immacolata, built in 1857 to celebrate Pope Pius IX's declaration of the Immaculate Conception.

★ Top Tips

o No picnics on the steps, please! It is forbidden to eat and drink or 'shout, squall and sing' on the beautifully restored staircase. Doing so risks a fine of up to €500.

o A prime photo op is during the springtime festival Mostra delle Azalee, held late March/early April, when hundreds of vases of bright pink azaleas in bloom adorn the steps.

o To skip the 135-step hike up, take the lift inside the Spagna metro station to the top.

✗ Take a Break

Play the Grand Tour tourist with morning or afternoon tea at 19th-century **Babington's Tea Rooms** (www.babingtons.com), at the foot of the Spanish Steps.

Watch the sun set over the steps from the fabulous ringside terrace of cocktail bar **Il Palazzetto**.

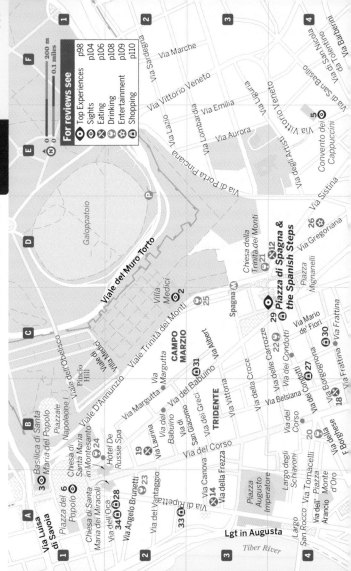

Tridente, Trevi & the Quirinale

For reviews see

◉	Top Experiences	p98
◉	Sights	p104
⊗	Eating	p106
⊕	Drinking	p108
⊕	Entertainment	p109
⊗	Shopping	p110

200 m
0.1 miles

Via Marche
Via Sardegna
Via Vittorio Veneto
Via Lombardia
Via Emilia
Via Aurora
Via Liguria
Via Lazio
Via Vittorio Veneto
Via di Porta Pinciana

Via degli Artisti
Convento dei
Cappuccini 5 ⊗
Via di San Nicola da Tolentino
Via di San Basilio
Via Barberini

Via Sistina

Viale del Muro Torto

Galoppatoio
P

Pincio Hill
Viale dell'Obelisco
Viale di Napoleone I
Piazzale
Viale D'Annunzio

Villa
Medici ◉2
Viale di
Villa Medici
Viale Trinità dei Monti

Chiesa della
Trinità dei Monti
21 ⊗ ⊗12
Via Gregoriana
26 ⊗
Piazza
Mignanelli

Spagna Ⓜ

9 ⊗
25

◉ Piazza di Spagna &
the Spanish Steps
29 ⊕

Via Mario
de' Fiori
30 ⊕

CAMPO
MARZIO

Via Margutta
Via
Via del Babuino
Via Alibert
Via delle Carrozze
22 ⊗
Via delle Carrozze
Via dei Condotti
Via dei Condotti 27 ⊕
Via Bocca di Leone
18 ⊗
Via Frattina
Via Frattina

Basilica di Santa
Maria del Popolo 3◉
Piazza del
Popolo ◉6
Chiesa di
Santa Maria
in Montesanto
Chiesa di Santa
Maria dei Miracoli
34 ⊕ ⊕28
Via dell'Oca
Via Angelo Brunetti
24 ⊗
Hotel De
Russie Spa
Via del Corso
19 ⊗
23 ⊗
Via Laurina
Via del Vantaggio
Via di Ripetta
33 ⊕
Via Canova
Via dei Greci
Via di San Giacomo
Via della Croce
Via della Frezza
14 ⊗
Via Vittoria

TRIDENTE

Via Belsiana
Via del
Corso
20 ⊗
Via della
F Borghese

Piazza Augusto
Imperatore
Largo degli
Schiavoni
Via Tomacelli
Largo
San Rocco
Via dell'
Arancio Piazza Monte
d'Oro

Lgt in Augusta
Tiber River

Via Luisa
di Savoia

N

1
2
3
4

A B C D E F

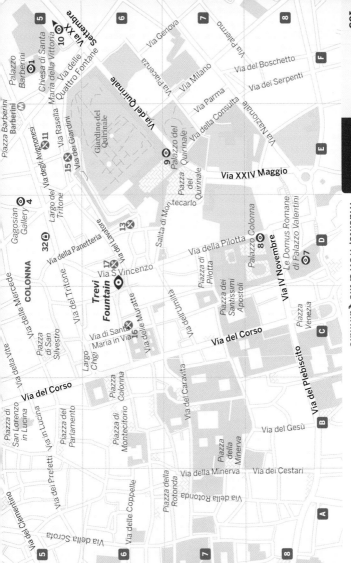

Sights

Palazzo Barberini
GALLERY

1 MAP P102, F5

Commissioned to celebrate the Barberini family's rise to papal power, this sumptuous baroque palace impresses even before you view its breathtaking art collection. Many high-profile architects worked on it, including rivals Bernini and Borromini: the former contributed a square staircase, the latter a helicoidal one. Amid the masterpieces on display, don't miss Filippo Lippi's *Annunciazione e due donatori* (Annunciation with Two Donors; 1440–45) and Pietro da Cortona's ceiling fresco *Il Trionfo della Divina Provvidenza* (The Triumph of Divine Providence; 1632–39). (www.barberinicorsini.org)

Villa Medici
PALACE

2 MAP P102, C2

Built for Cardinal Ricci da Montepulciano in 1540, this sumptuous Renaissance palace was purchased by Ferdinando de' Medici in 1576 and remained in Medici hands until 1801, when Napoleon acquired it for the French Academy. Guided tours (1½ hours) in multiple languages take in the sculpture-filled gardens and orchard, a garden studio exquisitely frescoed by Jacopo Zucchi in 1577 and the cardinal's private apartments. Note the pieces of ancient Roman sculpture from the Ara Pacis embedded in the villa's walls. (www.villamedici.it)

Basilica di Santa Maria del Popolo
BASILICA

3 MAP P102, A1

This is one of Rome's richest Renaissance churches, with a particularly impressive collection of art, including two Caravaggios: the *Conversion of St Paul* (1600–01) and the *Crucifixion of St Peter* (1601). These are in the 16th-century **Cerasi Chapel** to the left of the main altar. Other fine works include Caracci's *Assumption of the Virgin* (c 1660) in the same chapel and multiple frescoes by Pinturicchio; look for his 1484–90 *Adoration of the Christ Child* in the **Della Rovere Chapel**. (www.facebook.com/basilicasantamariadelpopolo)

Gagosian Gallery
GALLERY

4 MAP P102, D5

The Rome branch of Larry Gagosian's contemporary art empire has hosted the big names of contemporary art since it opened in 2007: Cy Twombly, Damien Hirst and Lawrence Weiner, to name only a few. The gallery is housed in an artfully converted 1920s bank, and was designed by Roman architect Firouz Galdo and Englishman Caruso St John. (www.gagosian.com)

Convento dei Cappuccini
MUSEUM

5 MAP P102, E4

This Capucin complex safeguards Rome's strangest sight: a crypt where everything from the picture frames to the light fittings is made of the bones of 3700 Capuchin monks as a macabre *memento mori* (reminder of death). Created between 1732 and 1775, six chapels line a 30m-long passageway, each named after the signature bone used to decorate it (The Crypt of the Pelvises, for example). There's even an arch crafted from skulls, vertebrae used as fleurs-de-lis, and light fixtures made of femurs. (www. cappucciniviaveneto.it)

Piazza del Popolo   PIAZZA

6 ◎ MAP P102, A1

This massive piazza was laid out in 1538 to provide a grandiose entrance to what was then Rome's main northern gateway. Standing sentinel at its southern approach are Carlo Rainaldi's twin 17th-century churches, **Chiesa di Santa Maria dei Miracoli** and **Basilica di Santa Maria in Montesanto**. In the centre, the 36m-high obelisk was brought by Augustus from ancient Egypt.

Le Domus Romane di Palazzo Valentini   ARCHAEOLOGICAL SITE

7 ◎ MAP P102, D8

Underneath a mansion that's been the seat of the Province of Rome since 1873 lie the archaeological remains of several lavish Roman houses. The excavated fragments have been turned into a fascinating virtual tour that takes you around the dwellings, complete with sound effects, vividly projected frescoes and glimpses of ancient life as it might have been

lived in the area. It's genuinely thrilling. The multilingual tours rotate every 30 minutes in Italian, English, French, German and Spanish. Book ahead during holiday periods. (www.palazzovalentini.it)

Palazzo Colonna   GALLERY

8 ◎ MAP P102, D8

The guided tours of this opulent palace introduce visitors to the residence and art collection of the patrician Colonna family. The largest private palace in Rome, it has a formal garden, multiple reception rooms and a grandiose baroque Great Hall built to honour Marcantonio II Colonna, a hero of the 1571 Battle of Lepanto. Guides recount plenty of anecdotes about family members, including fascinating Maria Mancini Mazzarino, a feisty favourite of Louis XIV of France. (www.galleriacolonna.it)

Palazzo del Quirinale   PALACE

9 ◎ MAP P102, E7

Perched atop the Quirinale Hill, one of Rome's seven hills, this former papal summer residence has been home to the Italian head of state since 1946. Originally commissioned by Pope Gregory XIII (r 1572–85), it was built and added to over 150 years by architects including Ottaviano Mascherino, Domenico Fontana, Francesco Borromini, Gian Lorenzo Bernini and Carlo Maderno. Guided tours (in Italian only) of its grand reception rooms should be booked at least five days ahead by telephone, or online. (www.quirinale.it)

Chiesa di Santa Maria della Vittoria

CHURCH

10 ◉ MAP P102, F5

Designed by Carlo Maderno, this modest church is an unlikely setting for an extraordinary work of art – Bernini's extravagant and sexually charged *Santa Teresa trafitta dall'amore di Dio* (Ecstasy of St Teresa). This daring sculpture depicts Teresa, engulfed in the folds of a flowing cloak, floating in ecstasy on a cloud while a teasing angel pierces her repeatedly with a golden arrow. It's in the fourth chapel on the north side.

Eating

Colline Emiliane

EMILIAN €€

11 🍴 MAP P102, E5

Serving sensational regional cuisine from Emilia-Romagna, this restaurant has been operated by the Latini family since 1931. Our recommendations when eating here: start with the *antipasti della casa* (€26 for two persons) and progress to pasta. Seasonal delights include white truffles in winter and fresh porcini mushrooms in spring, but the menu is delectable whatever the season. (www.collineemiliane.com)

Imàgo

ITALIAN €€€

12 🍴 MAP P102, D3

Even in a city of great views, the panoramas from the Michelin-starred romantic rooftop restaurant at **Hotel Hassler Roma** are special, extending over a sea of roofs to the great dome of St Peter's Basilica; request the corner table. Complementing the views are the bold, modern Italian creations from talented young chef Andrea Antonini who plays expertly with texture and flavour. Tasting menus range from €130 to €170. (www.imagorestaurant.com)

Piccolo Arancio

TRATTORIA €€

13 🍴 MAP P102, D6

In a 'hood riddled with tourist traps, this backstreet eatery – tucked inside a little house next to grandiose Palazzo Scanderberg – stands out. The kitchen mixes Roman classics with more contemporary options and, unusually, includes lots of seafood choices – the *linguini alla pescatora* (handmade pasta with shellfish and baby tomatoes) and fried fillet of *baccalà* (cod) are simply sensational. (www.piccoloarancio.it)

La Buca di Ripetta

TRATTORIA €€

14 🍴 MAP P102, A3

Popular with locals, who know a good thing when they taste it, this trattoria serves traditional dishes with a refreshingly refined execution. Octopus carpaccio, gnocchi with courgette flowers and ravioli stuffed with ricotta and pear are just some of the imaginative dishes on the menu. Service is also super friendly and efficient, and they will readily help with wine pairings. (www.facebook.com/LaBucadiRipetta)

Hostaria Romana TRATTORIA €€

15 🍴 MAP P102, E5

Beloved of locals and tourists alike, this bustling place in Trevi is everything an Italian trattoria should be. Order an antipasto or pasta (excellent) and then move onto a main – traditional Roman dishes including *saltimbocca* (pan-fried, prosciutto-wrapped veal escalopes) and *trippa* (tripe) are on offer, as are lots of grilled meats. If lucky, your meal may be rounded off with complimentary *biscotti*. (www.hostariaromana.it)

Pane e Salami SANDWICHES €

16 🍴 MAP P102, C6

A hole-in-the-wall that does what it says on the tin: huge platters of cheese and salami and top-notch sandwiches made with fresh focaccia. These aren't your normal sandwiches, but taste sensations filled with creamy ricotta, spicy salami and grilled fresh vegetables. There's a tiny outdoor seating area and you can order a good glass of wine to round things off. (www.facebook.com/panesalameroma)

Il Chianti TUSCAN €€

17 🍴 MAP P102, D6

This pretty ivy-clad place specialises in Tuscan-style wine and food. Cosy up inside its bottle-lined interior or grab a table on the street terrace and dig into Tuscan favourites including crostini (toasts with toppings), *taglieri* (platters of cheese and cured meats), hearty soups, handmade pasta and Florence's iconic T-bone steak. (www.chiantiosteriatoscana.it)

Palazzo Barberini (p104)

Relaxing Spa Time

If you're looking for some me-time after hours of dazzling Roman sightseeing, consider booking a treatment at one of the two top hotel spas at the **Hotel de Russie** (Map p102; www.roccofortehotels.com) or the **Hotel Hassler Roma** (www.hotelhasslerroma.com).

The former has a gorgeous mosaic-lined salt-water hydro-pool, a Finnish sauna and steam room, as well as an array of treatments from shiatsu to deep-tissue massage. The latter offers a sauna and steam bath alongside facials and body treatments using the hotel's signature Amorvero products.

Ginger
BRASSERIE €€

18 🍴 MAP P102, B4

This buzzy white space is a popular all-day dining spot. The focus is on organic Slow Food dishes using seasonal appellation d'origine protégée (AOP) ingredients; healthy eats are a focus, with freshly made sandwiches, meal-sized salads, energy bowls, cold-pressed juices and fruit smoothies. The spacious pavement terrace has winter heaters for year-round use. (www.gingersaporiesalute.com)

Fatamorgana Corso
GELATO €

19 🍴 MAP P102, B2

Ambrosial flavours abound at this artisanal *gelateria* near the Spanish Steps, all made using the finest seasonal ingredients. There are several other branches around town. (www.gelateriafatamorgana.com)

Drinking

Zuma Bar
COCKTAIL BAR

20 🚇 MAP P102, B4

One way to experience the fabulous Fendi fashion house is to reserve for drinks or dinner on the rooftop of Palazzo Fendi. Few cocktail bars in Rome are as sleek, hip or achingly sophisticated as this. City views are fantastic and cocktails mix exciting flavours like shiso with juniper berries, elderflower and prosecco, besides which you can order delicious Japanese izakaya tasting plates. DJs spin Zuma playlists at weekends. (www.zumarestaurant.com)

Hassler Bar
COCKTAIL BAR

21 🚇 MAP P102, D3

The Hotel Hassler's iconic 1940s-style cocktail bar is loved by high-fliers and celebrities alike for its clubby crimson leather-and-dark wood interiors and excellent cocktails. This drinking den is only open between October and April though. In summer, you have to make do with the Palm Court, a stunning courtyard garden with a sweeping, clam-shaped, chrome-and-glass fountain-bar that bookends an elegant outdoor patio where you can also dine on light bistrot fare. (www.hotelhasslerroma.com)

Antico Caffè Greco

CAFE

22 🏛 MAP P102, C4

Casanova, Goethe, Wagner, Keats, Byron, Shelley and Baudelaire were all regulars at Rome's oldest and most elegant cafe, which opened in 1760. Prices reflect this amazing heritage: pay nearly four times more if you sit at a table rather than stand at the bar. If you opt for the latter, be sure to exit through the elegant interior salons to admire the furnishings. (www. facebook.com/AnticoCaffeGreco)

Buccone

WINE BAR

23 🏛 MAP P102, A2

Step in under the faded gilt-and-mirrored sign and you'll feel as though you've gone back in time. Once a coach house, then a tavern, this building became a wine shop in the 1960s, furnished with 19th-century antiques and lined with around a thousand Italian wines. You can sample some of the offerings alongside a light lunch or at aperitivo hour with mixed plates of cured meat and cheese. (www.enotecabuccone.com)

Stravinskij Bar

BAR

24 🏛 MAP P102, B1

Can't afford to stay at the celeb-magnet **Hotel de Russie**? Then splash out on a drink at its swish bar. There are sofas inside, but the sunny courtyard is the fashionable choice, with sun-shaded tables overlooked by terraced gardens. In the best *dolce vita* style, it's perfect for a pricey cocktail or beer accompanied by appropriately posh snacks. Dress up and make a reservation at weekends. (www.roccofortehotels.com/hotels-and-resorts/hotel-de-russie)

Caffè Ciampini

CAFE

25 🏛 MAP P102, C3

A short walk from the top of the Spanish Steps towards the Pincio Hill Gardens, this cafe and restaurant has a garden-party vibe, with green trelliswork and orange trees framing its white-clothed tables. There are lovely views, and the gelato – particularly the *tartufo al cioccolato* (chocolate truffle) – is renowned. The restaurants serves bistro classics and pizzas. (https://ristoranteciampini.com)

Entertainment

Gregory's Jazz Club

JAZZ

26 ⭐ MAP P102, D4

If Gregory's were a tone of voice, it'd be husky: unwind over a whisky in the downstairs bar, then unwind some more on squashy sofas upstairs to slinky live jazz and swing, with quality local performers who also like to hang out here. (www. gregorysjazz.com)

Shopping

Federico Buccellati
JEWELLERY

27 🅐 MAP P102, C4

Run today by the third generation of one of Italy's most prestigious silver- and goldsmiths, this historical shop opened in 1926. Everything is hand- crafted and often delicately engraved with decorative flowers, leaves and nature-inspired motifs. Don't miss the Silver Salon on the 1st floor showcasing some original silverware and jewellery pieces by grandfather Mario. (www.buccellati.com)

Bomba
CLOTHING

28 🅐 MAP P102, A2

Opened by designer Cristina Bomba over four decades ago, this gor- geous boutique is now operated by her fashion-designing children Ca- terina (womenswear) and Michele (menswear). Using the highest- quality fabrics, their creations are tailored in the next-door atelier (peek through the front window); woollens are produced at a factory just outside the city. Pricey but oh so worth it. (https://atelierbomba.com)

Sermoneta
FASHION & ACCESSORIES

29 🅐 MAP P102, C4

Buying leather gloves in Rome is a rite of passage for some, and the city's most famous glove-seller opposite the Spanish Steps is the place to go. Choose from a kaleido- scopic range of leather and suede gloves lined with silk and cashmere. An expert assistant will size up your hand in a glance and supply the cor- rect fit. (www.sermonetagloves.com)

Fausto Santini
SHOES

30 🅐 MAP P102, C4

Rome's best-known shoe designer, Fausto Santini is famous for his be- guilingly simple, architectural shoe designs, realised in boots and shoes made with butter-soft leather. Col- ours are beautiful and the quality is impeccable. Seek out the end-of-line **discount shop** in Monti to source a bargain. (www.faustosantini.com)

Gente
FASHION & ACCESSORIES

31 🅐 MAP P102, C3

This multilabel boutique was the first in Rome to bring all the big- name luxury designers – Italian, French and otherwise – under one roof. Its vast emporium-styled space remains an essential stop for every serious fashionista. Labels include Dolce & Gabbana, Prada, Alexander McQueen, Sergio Rossi and Missoni. (www.genteroma.com)

La Rinascente
DEPARTMENT STORE

32 🅐 MAP P102, D5

This upmarket department store is famous in Italy and beyond for its trend-setting collections and interesting array of international brands. There's also designer homewares, a huge food hall with eateries and a rooftop cocktail bar – the **Up Sunset Bar** – which has panoramic views of Rome and is open all day. (www.rinascente.it)

Fabulous Shopping Streets

Tridente is Rome's premier shopping district and is packed with all manner of shops from big luxury brands to independent boutiques. The sales are on in January and July.

Via del Corso (Map p102) Once Via Flaminia, the main street in ancient Rome, and now the main shopping drag. It is lined with big brands, savvy streetwear, homeware and food specialists.

Via dei Condotti (Map p102) Rome's smartest strip, home to the biggest Italian and international brands, including the gorgeous Fendi flagship store. At the eastern end is Caffè Greco, a favourite rendezvous of 18th- and 19th-century writers.

Via Frattina (Map p102) The place fashionistas come to score bargains and one-of-a-kind pieces from interesting independents like Fausto Santini, Falconeri and Nashi Argan.

Via Margutta (Map p102) Lined with galleries, Rome's prettiest cobbled lane has long been associated with artists: Picasso worked at No 54, Audrey Hepburn and Gregory Peck flirted at No 51 in the film *Roman Holiday*, and film director Federico Fellini lived at No 110 until his death in 1993.

Via del Babuino (Map p102) Luxury brands such as Chanel and Moschino, mixed in with outlet stores for more affordable options. The famous Hotel de Russie is also located here.

Mia Home Design Gallery

HOMEWARES

33 MAP P102, A2

An old palazzo provides the perfect space to showcase the sophisticated and eclectic collection of design items, homewares and textiles pulled together by three design-mad friends, Marianna, Emilia and Maria. They source their treasures from a mix of small Italian and international designers who stand out for their originality. (https://galleriamia.it)

Artisanal Cornucopia

CONCEPT STORE

34 MAP P102, A2

One of several stylish boutiques on Via dell'Oca, Elif Sallorenzo's chic concept store showcases exclusive handmade pieces by Italian designers alongside her own clothing designs and objects from around the globe. There are loads of bags, shoes, candles, jewellery pieces, homewares and other objects to covet. (www.artisanalcornucopia.com)

Worth a Trip 👀
Marvel at the Borghese Gallery

Cardinal Scipione Borghese, the powerful nephew of Pope Paul V, had this exquisite villa built in 1613, amid his family's landscaped parklands; it was remodelled in the 18th century to showcase the splendid collection begun by the cardinal and added to by subsquent descendants. He had deep pockets and a keen eye for talent, collecting masterworks by artists such as Gian Lorenzo Bernini, Caravaggio, Titian, Raphael and Rubens.

http://galleriaborghese.beniculturali.it

The Villa

The museum's collection was begun by the ruthless Cardinal Scipione Borghese (1577–1633), the savviest and most powerful art collector of his day. It was originally housed in the cardinal's residence near St Peter's, but in the 1620s he had it transferred to a new villa just outside Porta Pinciana. It remained here, in the Casino Borghese, whose interiors were remodelled by architect Antonio Asprucci in the 18th century to celebrate the Borghese family and showcase the collection.

Ground Floor

Stairs lead up to a portico flanking the grand entrance hall, decorated with 4th-century floor mosaics of fighting gladiators and a 2nd-century *Satiro Combattente* (Fighting Satyr). High on the wall is a gravity-defying bas-relief of a horse and rider falling into the void (*Marco Curzio a Cavallo*) by Pietro Bernini (Gian Lorenzo's father).

The statuesque scene-stealer in **Sala I** is Antonio Canova's daring depiction of Napoleon's sister, Paolina Bonaparte Borghese, reclining topless as *Venere vincitrice* (1805–08). The pillowy stone mattress contained a mechanism that made the sculpture rotate.

Further on, in **Sala III**, Bernini's *Apollo e Dafne* (1622–25), one of a series depicting pagan myths, captures the exact moment Daphne's hands start morphing into leaves. Bernini intended that viewers should approach from the right, so that the story would be slowly revealed. **Sala IV** is home to Bernini's unsettling masterpiece *Ratto di Proserpina* (1621–22), showing the moment Pluto abducts Persephone, a smirk on his face as she recoils in terror. Bernini's virtuosity here is incredible: look at Pluto's hand pressing into the seemingly soft flesh of Persephone's thigh.

★ **Top Tips**

○ To limit numbers, visitors are admitted at two-hourly intervals – book your ticket well in advance.

○ Hire a bike from one of the bike stands in Villa Borghese; ebikes are available from some stands. You'll need to leave ID.

○ The 'secret gardens' to the gallery are sometimes open in summer for guided tours. Check the website.

✕ **Take a Break**

The gallery has a sleek little cafe in the basement, or you can head through Villa Borghese to **Caffè delle Arti**, a grand cafe-restaurant with a large and lovely sun-shaded terrace, serving coffee and meals at La Galleria Nazionale.

★ **Getting There**

🚌 Bus 53 or 910 to Via Pinciana.

Ⓜ From Spagna or Flaminio (line A) you can walk up to Villa Borghese.

Caravaggio dominates **Sala VIII**. There's a dissipated-looking self-portrait *Bacchino malato* (Sick Bacchus; 1592–95), thought to be so-named as Caravaggio painted it following a stint in hospital; and *San Giovanni Battista* (St John the Baptist; 1609–10), probably Caravaggio's last work, painted in Naples as he awaited a papal pardon. There's also the *Ragazzo con Canestro di Frutta* (Boy with a Basket of Fruit; 1593–95) with the fruit painted with extraordinary attention to detail, and the dramatic *Davide con la Testa di Golia* (David with the Head of Goliath; 1609–10) – Goliath's severed head is apparently another self-portrait and the work a thank you for Cardinal Scipione's assistance in Caravaggio avoiding a death sentence for committing murder in 1606.

Pinacoteca

Upstairs, the picture gallery contains numerous Renaissance masterpieces. Don't miss Raphael's extraordinary *La Deposizione di Cristo* (The Deposition; 1507), with its harmonious composition in an idealised landscape, in **Sala IX**, and his *Dama con Liocorno* (Lady with a Unicorn; 1506); the unicorn was a symbol of chastity. In the same room is Fra Bartolomeo's superb *Adorazione del Bambino* (Adoration of the Christ Child; 1495), influenced by Leonardo da Vinci, and Perugino's *Madonna con Bambino* (Madonna and Child; first quarter of the 16th century) with an Umbrian backdrop.

Villa Borghese gardens

Next door in **Sala X**, Correggio's *Danäe* (1530–31) shares the room with a willowy Venus, as portrayed by German artist Lucas Cranach in his *Venere e Amore che Reca Il Favo do Miele* (Venus and Cupid with Honeycomb; 1531).

In Sala XIV you can see two revealing marble busts of Cardinal Scipione by Bernini. **Sala XVIII** is home to two works by Rubens, including *Susanna e I Vecchioni* (Susanna and the Elders; 1605–07).

A fitting highlight on which to finish is Titian's early masterpiece *Amor Sacro e Amor Profano* (Sacred and Profane Love; 1514), in **Sala XX**, where the red and white colours are thought to symbolise the marital attributes of chastity and passion.

DFLC PRINTS/SHUTTERSTOCK ©

Villa Borghese

Villa Borghese

Extending for about 80 hectares around the museum, **Villa Borghese** is Rome's Central Park, shaded by elegant Mediterranean pines and scattered by historic sculpture, with a lake, a theatre and several museums.

As well as Rome's **Bioparco** (www.bioparco.it) zoo, you'll find **Museo Nazionale Etrusco di Villa Giulia** (www.villagiulia.beniculturali.it), showcasing Italy's finest collection of Etruscan and pre-Roman treasures, and **La Galleria Nazionale** (http://lagallerianazionale.com), with a superlative collection of modern art.

Auditorium Parco della Musica

The hub of Rome's cultural scene, the **Auditorium Parco della Musica** (www.auditorium.com) is the capital's premier concert venue. Its three concert halls and 3000-seat open-air arena stage everything from classical music concerts to jazz gigs, public lectures and film screenings.

Explore

Monti & Esquilino

Monti (meaning 'mountains') spreads across three hills – Esquilino, Viminale and the Quirinale – and was once Suburra, ancient Rome's red light district, and Julius Caesar's home until the age of 37. Today, it's peppered with Airbnbs, small boutiques, bars and restaurants. It's not as hip with locals as it was, but it's still a lively, beguiling place for a browse. Esquilino is one of Rome's seven hills and comprises the sprawling area around Stazione Termini.

The Short List

○ **Palazzo Massimo alle Terme (p118)** *Seeing glorious ancient Roman frescoes, relics from Caligula's barge, and the extraordinary 'Boxer' at this unsung, under-visited museum.*

○ **Monti** *Enjoying an amble and an aperitivo in this bohemian-feeling neighbourhood.*

○ **Basilica di Santa Maria Maggiore (p123)** *Feeling humbled by awesome Byzantine and baroque splendours.*

○ **Domus Aurea (p123)** *Exploring the subterranean remains of Nero's city-scale golden palace.*

Getting There & Around

Ⓜ Cavour (line B) for Monti; Termini (lines A and B), Castro Pretorio (line B) and Vittorio Emanuele (line A) for Esquilino.

🚌 Termini is Rome's main hub, with buses heading citywide from here. Access Monti from stops on Via Nazionale or Via Cavour.

Neighbourhood Map on p122

Basilica di Santa Maria Maggiore (p123) NATTEE CHALERMTIRAGOOL/SHUTTERSTOCK ©

Top Experience

Discover Palazzo Massimo alle Terme

One of Rome's finest museums, in a convent turned hospital turned school, later becoming this under-visited yet extraordinary branch of the Museo Nazionale. To see its wonders when you're fresh, start your visit on the 2nd floor; the frescoes and mosaics here show how the interiors of grand ancient Roman villas really looked.

◉ MAP P122, D2

www.
museonazionaleromano.
beniculturali.it

Villa Livia Frescoes

Room 2 on the second floor contains the sensational frescoed room from 1st-century BCE Villa Livia, which was the summer home of Augustus' wife Livia Drusilla, around 12km north of the city. This was the decor for a summer triclinium, a large living and dining area built half to keep it cool in summer. The plants are seasonally inconsistent and mildly exotic, including cypress, green oak, quince, pomegranate, myrtle and laurel trees, poppy, cabbage roses, chrysanthemum and violets, under a deep-blue, bird-filled sky. The villa was identified as Livia's in 1863 after being abandoned around the 5th century CE.

Villa Farnesina Frescoes

The other highlight of the second floor are the frescoes and mosaics of Villa Farnesina, discovered close to the banks of the Tiber and thought to have been built by General Marcus Vipsanius Agrippa, a close friend of Augustus. You can peer into the intimacy of the bedrooms decorated with images of the goddesses Artemis and Aphrodite, and a winter dining room painted black in accordance with the architectural writings of Vitruvius. A multimedia presentation gives an excellent idea of what the villa, which was rediscovered in Trastevere in 1879, would have looked like.

Ground & 1st Floors

The ground and 1st floors are devoted to sculpture. On the ground floor, the highlights are two 2nd-century-BCE Greek bronzes, *The Boxer* and *The Prince* (Room 7), and the beautiful Wounded Niobid (Room 6), with an arrow in her back.

Basement

The basement collection traces the history of the Roman Empire via coinage and is undergoing renovation.

★ **Top Tips**

○ Rent an audio guide at the main ticket desk for €5.

○ Combination tickets, valid for three days, also cover the Museo Nazionale Romano's other seats at: Terme di Diocleziano (p124), Palazzo Altemps (p66), **Museo dell'Arte Salvata** and **Crypta Balbi**.

✕ **Take a Break**

Set to the rear right-hand side of Termini station, the Mercato Centrale (p126) is a top-notch food court, with excellent pastries, *pizza al taglio* (by the slice), *supplì* (deep-fried rice balls) and much more.

To enjoy a coffee and decadently sweet Sicilian pastry, make the short walk to Dagnino (p128) in the nearby Esedra Arcade.

Monti's Bars & Boutiques

The first residential rione (district) established beyond the walls of the imperial city, Monti was once Suburra of ancient Rome, infamous for its brothels and sleaze. Today its name means, literally, 'mountains', and it still has an identity, but its narrow medieval streets are lined by mostly 18th-century, ivy-covered palazzi. Discovered by tourists in recent years, it feels rather like a mini-Trastevere, full of accommodation, restaurants and bars.

Walk Facts

Start La Bottega del Caffè; metro Cavour

End Blackmarket Hall; metro Cavour

Length 1.9km; one day

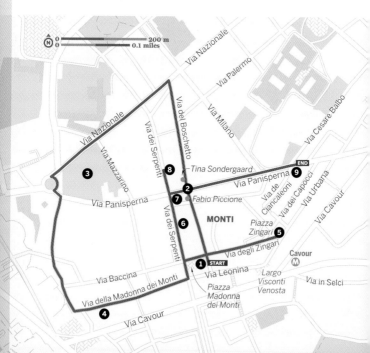

❶ Morning Coffee

Set on the eastern edge Piazza della Madonna dei Monti, which is centred on pretty Fontana dei Catecumeni, a fountain named for adults initiated to the Catholic Church, **La Bottega del Caffè** (p127) is a popular hub, with the prettiest outdoor seating.

❷ Boschetto Browse

Via del Boschetto is one of Monti's main drags, and is dotted by small independent boutiques such as the Scandi-tailoring of **Tina Sondergaard** (p129), or the glorious upcycled costume jewellery of **Fabio Piccione** (Via del Boschetto).

❸ Villa Aldobrandini

This area can feel hectic and without a green escape, so it's a relief to know that there is a tranquil bolthole just off Via Nazionale. This sculpture-dotted **garden** (p125) up some steps and in front of a 16th-century villa has a scattering of benches beneath perfumed orange trees.

❹ Pizza Refuel

Monti has some excellent *pizza al taglio* (by the slice) if you're on the move. However, make the time for a proper sit-down lunch at **Alle Carrette** (p125), which has seats out on a cobbled cul de sac and serves up thin-crust, piping-hot pizza. Service is friendly, prices are cheap and *fritti* (fried things) are excellent.

❺ Fatamorgana Gelato

This branch of the artisanal gelato-makers **Fatamorgana** (www.gelateriafatamorgana.com) is one of the best, and you can perch on the wall of the piazza to tuck into your delectable seasonal creation.

❻ Scouting Serpenti

Running parallel to Via del Boschetto, Via dei Serpenti is another great street for browsing boutiques, and has a view of the Colosseum from its southern end. As well as some small boutiques, it has one of the area's most popular vintage shops, **Pifebo** (p129).

❼ Ai Tre Scalini Tipple

A popular local hang-out since 1895, the **Ai Tre Scalini** (p127) is perennially packed with young Romans who catch up with friends over beers, glasses of wines and generous cheese and *salumi* platters. Those who can't cram in often adjourn to **Barzilai Bistro** (p128), opposite.

❽ Sundowner Spritz

There are several rooftops in Monti that are ideal for an aperitivo, including **Rooftop Spritzeria Monti** (https://en.bzarhotelandco.com), a popular, boho little rooftop with a view of a corner of the Colosseum at the end of the street if you crane to look.

❾ Late-night Monti

Blackmarket Hall (p128) is an offbeat venue on a Monti backstreet. It feels like a strung-out sitting room with lots of vintage armchairs and coffee tables. It's great for a drink and aperitivo, as well as to catch some of its regular live acts, which are often acoustic.

For reviews see

⊙	Top Experiences	p118
⊙	Sights	p123
⊗	Eating	p125
⊜	Drinking	p127
☆	Entertainment	p128
⌂	Shopping	p128

0 — 200 m
0 — 0.1 miles

Via delle Quattro Fontane

Via V E Orlando

Via Cernaia

3
Museo Nazionale
Romano: Terme
di Diocleziano

Via Modena

Ⓜ Repubblica

Viale L Einaudi

Viale Enrico de Nicola

Stazione
Termini
(50m)

Via del
Viminale

Largo di
Villa Peretti

Main Bus
Station

Via Firenze

Via Torino

19

Quirinale
(Quirinale
Hill)

Via Napoli

Piazza
Beniamino
Gigli

Via Massimo
d'Azeglio

Ⓜ Termini

**Museo Nazionale
Romano: Palazzo
Massimo alle Terme**

Via Amendola

Via Piacenza

Via Genova

Via Nazionale

Via Agostino Depretis

Piazza del
Viminale

ESQUILINO

⊗12

⊙ Palazzo delle
6 Esposizioni

Via Palermo

Ministero
dell'Interno

Piazza
dell'Esquilino

Via Farini

Via Gioberti

15
Villa Aldobrandini (225m)

Via Milano

Via Cesare Balbo

Via di Santa
Maria Maggiore

Basilica di
Santa Maria
Maggiore

⊗11

Via Urbana

Via Liberiana

Piazza
Santa Maria
1 Maggiore

⌂21

Via del Boschetto

Via Panisperna

Via dei Capocci

Via dei Quattro Cantoni

Via Paolina

Basilica
4⊙ di Santa
Prassede

16

⊗22

Via dei
Serpenti

Via Cimarra

18

Via Urbana

Via Cavour

Via dell'Olmata

Largo
Sant'
Alfonso

⊜13

⊜23

MONTI

Piazza
Zingari ⌂

⊗9

20

Via Sforza

Via San Martino
ai Monti

10
⊗

Piazza
Madonna
dei Monti **⊗14**

Via degli Zingari

Cavour
Ⓜ

Via Giovanni Lanza

Piazza
San Martino
ai Monti

Via dello
Statuto

Via Leonina

Largo
Visconti
Venosta

Via in Selci

Vino Roma

Via San Martino
ai Monti

8
⊗

Via Merulana

▲⊙7

Via Cavour

Via degli Annibaldi

5⊙ Basilica di
San Pietro
in Vincoli

Via delle Sette Sale

Via Eudossiana

Via della
Polveriera

Via delle
Terme di Tito

⊙**2**
Domus
Aurea

Parco di
Traiano

Viale del Monte Oppio

Via delle Terme di Traiano

Via Mecenate

Parco del
Colle Oppio

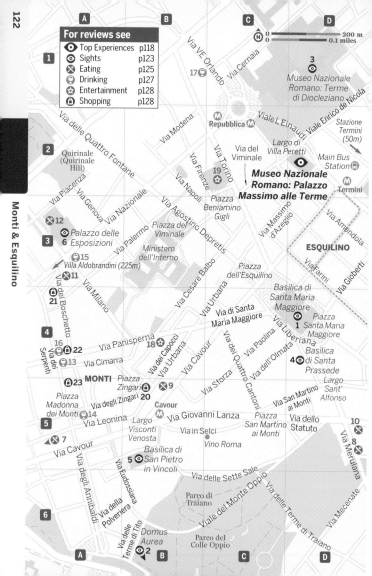

Sights

Basilica di Santa Maria Maggiore

BASILICA

1 ⊙ MAP P122, D4

One of Rome's four patriarchal basilicas, this 5th-century church stands on Esquiline Hill's summit, where snow is said to have miraculously fallen in the summer of 358 CE. Every year on 5 August, the event is recreated via a light show in Piazza Santa Maria Maggiore. The basilica is an architectural hybrid with 14th-century Romanesque campanile, Renaissance coffered ceiling, 18th-century baroque facade and an imposing baroque interior. Visit the loggia (€9) to get close to the glorious 13th-century mosaics.

Domus Aurea

ARCHAEOLOGICAL SITE

2 ⊙ MAP P122, B6

Nero had his Domus Aurea constructed after the fire of 64 CE (which he is rumoured to have started to clear the area). Named after the gold that lined its facade and interiors, it was more like a city than a house. Today, it's a rare chance to see entirely preserved Roman rooms and hallways, though sadly most of the frescoes have deteriorated and are barely visible. There's some excellent virtual reality and projections to indicate how the ruins would once have looked. You need to book tours ahead online. Enter from Via Labicana. (Golden House; www. coopculture.it)

Domus Aurea

Museo Nazionale Romano: Terme di Diocleziano

MUSEUM

3 ⊙ MAP P122, D1

The baths that Termini station is named after, this huge complex could accommodate 3000 people, and was one of ancient Rome's largest. Now a museum on Rome's prehistory and epigraphy, its exhibits provide a fascinating insight into ancient Roman life, covering cults such as Mithraism, ancient altars and tombstone inscriptions. Don't overlook the vast and well-preserved baths hall, to the left as you approach the museum, now a temporary exhibition space.

In the main museum, the large 16th-century cloister was built as part of the charterhouse of **Santa Maria degli Angeli e dei Martiri** (www.santamariadegliangeliroma.it)

Basilica di Santa Prassede

CHURCH

4 ⊙ MAP P122, D4

Famous for its brilliant blue and gold Byzantine mosaics, preserved in their original state, this small 9th-century church is dedicated to St Praxedes, an early Christian heroine who hid Christians fleeing persecution and buried those she couldn't save in a well. The position of the well is now marked by a marble disc on the floor of the nave.

Basilica di Santa Prassede

SIR FRANCIS CANKER PHOTOGRAPHY/GETTY IMAGES ©

Basilica di San Pietro in Vincoli

BASILICA

5 MAP P122, B5

Pilgrims and art lovers flock to this 5th-century basilica to see Michelangelo's colossal *Moses* sculpture (1505) and to see the chains that are said to have bound St Peter when he was imprisoned in the Carcere Mamertino ('in Vincoli' means 'in Chains'). Also of note is a 7th-century mosaic icon of St Sebastian. Access is via a steep flight of steps leading up from Via Cavour and passing under a low arch.

Palazzo delle Esposizioni

CULTURAL CENTRE

6 MAP P122, A3

This huge neoclassical palace was built in 1882 as an exhibition centre, though it has since served as headquarters for the Italian Communist Party, a mess hall for Allied servicemen, a polling station and even a public loo. Nowadays it's a splendid cultural hub, with cathedral-scale exhibition spaces hosting blockbuster art exhibitions. There's a large art bookshop, a cafe with a small courtyard, and the swish, glass-roofed Antonello Colonna Open (p126) restaurant. (www.palazzoesposizioni.it)

Eating

Alle Carrette

PIZZA €

7 MAP P122, A5

Authentic pizza, super-thin and swiftly cooked in a wood-fired

Villa Aldobrandini

If you're in need of a breather around Via Nazionale or are in search of somewhere for a picnic, follow Via Mazzarino off the main road and walk up the steps, past 2nd-century ruins, to **Villa Aldobrandini** (Map p122, A3), a graceful, sculpture-dotted garden with gravel paths and benches beneath fragrant orange trees, palms and camellias.

oven, is what keeps locals and tourists filling this traditional Roman pizzeria, with tables outside on a cobbled cul de sac, friendly service and good *fritti* (fried things). Romans pile in here at weekends for good reason – it's cheap, friendly and delicious. (www.facebook.com/allecarrette)

Panella

BAKERY €

8 MAP P122, D5

Freshly baked pastries, fruit tartlets, *pizza al taglio* (pizza by the slice) and focaccia fill display cases in this famous bakery, and there's also a *tavola calda* ('hot table') where an array of hot dishes is on offer. Order at the counter and eat at bar stools between shelves of gourmet groceries, or sit on the terrace for waiter service. (www.panellaroma.com)

Termini Food Hall

A gourmet food hall for hungry travellers at Stazione Termini, the **Mercato Centrale** (Map p122; www.mercatocentrale.it/roma) with its vaulted 1930s ceiling hosts stalls selling good-quality fast food and fresh produce. Consider purchasing a *panino* filled with artisanal cheese from **Beppe Giovali**; a slice of focaccia or pizza from **Gabriele Bonci**; or a Chianina burger from **Enrico Lagorio**. A *birreria* (beer house) sells craft beer.

Zia Rosetta
SANDWICHES €

9 MAP P122, B5

Grab a pew at a marble-topped table at 'Aunt Rosetta' and select from its wide range of gourmet *rosette*, small, crusty, almost hollow rolls with a distinctive cross shape on the top, creatively stuffed with delectable combinations, such as ham and fig, or veal with tuna sauce, green beans and capers. You can go for mini or classic sizes. There are gluten-free options and freshly squeezed juices. (www.ziarosetta.com)

Pasticceria Regoli
BAKERY €

10 MAP P122, D5

At weekends a queue marks the entrance to this elegant chande-lier-lit *pasticceria,* much-loved since 1916. Its *crostate* (latticed jam tarts) are a tangy fruit delight, as are its berry-topped *crostatine fragoline di bosco*. There's a ticketed queueing system. (www.pasticceriaregoli.com)

La Barrique
OSTERIA €€

11 MAP P122, A3

As popular with local residents as it is with tourists, this is a bottle-lined neighbourhood enoteca that also offers a menu of creative daily dishes inspired by what's fresh at the local markets. The interesting wine list is mostly sourced from small producers and includes plenty of natural wines. (www.facebook.com/la.barrique.94)

Antonello Colonna Open
GASTRONOMY €€€

12 MAP P122, A3

Spectacularly set on the covered terrace to the rear of Palazzo delle Esposizioni, Antonello Colonna's restaurant is on the mezzanine floor of the restaurant, all of which is covered by a wow-factor all-glass roof.

Cuisine is new Roman – innovative takes on traditional dishes, cooked with wit and flair. On sunny days, dine al fresco on the rooftop terrace. There are cheaper weekday lunches in the less-formal lunchtime restaurant. (www.antonellocolonna.it)

Drinking

Ai Tre Scalini
WINE BAR

13 MAP P122, A4

A firm favourite since 1895, the 'Three Steps' is inevitably packed with young patrons spilling out of its two-room interior, and it now has added some streetside tables. It's a perfect spot to enjoy an afternoon drink or a simple meal of cheese, salami and home-style mains (including vegan and gluten-free options), washed down with excellent choices of beer or wine by the glass. (www.aitrescalini.org)

La Bottega del Caffè
CAFE

14 MAP P122, A5

On one of Rome's prettiest squares, La Bottega del Caffè – named after a comedy by Carlo Goldoni – is the hotspot in Monti for lingering over excellent coffee, drinks, snacks (sandwiches and panini €3 to €6) and lunch or dinner. Heaters in winter ensure balmy al fresco action year-round.

Terrazza Monti
BAR

15 MAP P122, A3

A great, if pricey, escape from the frenetic bustle of busy Via Nazionale at ground level, this rooftop terrace is open all day and has great views across the Monti rooftops. It's the kind of place that plays lounge music and feels like a hotel bar, but it's still ideal for a fancy aperitivo or an evening drink, completely switching it up from the pace down at street level. (www.aghotels.it)

Ai Tre Scalini

Barzilai Bistrot

WINE BAR

16 MAP P122, A4

Opposite Monti's much-loved Ai Tre Scalini, this bohemian bar-bistro accommodates the people who can't squeeze in over the road but are seeking a similarly casual place to enjoy a drink and something to eat. Sit at one of the tables under the huge chandelier or stand at the bar; when it's full, they're happy to serve drinks through the window.

Dagnino

CAFE

17 MAP P122, B1

Secreted in the Esedra Arcade near Piazza della Repubblica, this cafe has retained its original 1960s decor, including murals – you'll feel like you're entering a time warp when enjoying a coffee and one of the Sicilian-style treats (*cannoli*,

Wine Tasting

With beautifully appointed century-old cellars and a chic tasting studio, **Vino Roma** (Map p122, C5; www.vinoroma. com) guides both novices and wine enthusiasts in the basics of Italian wine under the knowledgable stewardship of sommelier Hande Leimer and her expert team. Also on offer are a wine-and-cheese dinner (€65) with cheeses, cold cuts and perfect pairings, and bespoke three-hour food tours. Book online.

cassatas etc) for which it is famous, or a gelato, which is also a good call.

Entertainment

Blackmarket Hall

LIVE MUSIC

18 MAP P122, B4

One of Monti's best bar-venues, this former monastery has a series of rooms furnished by vintage armchairs and tables, and feels rather like drinking in the ramshackle sitting room of a stately home. There's often live jazz and acoustic performances – check the website for details. (www.blackmarkethall.com)

Teatro dell'Opera di Roma

OPERA

19 MAP P122, C2

Rome's foremost opera house, aka Teatro Costanzi, has a Fascist 1920s exterior, red-and-gilt interior, and an impressive history: it premiered both Puccini's *Tosca* and Mascagni's *Cavalleria rusticana*. Opera and ballet performances are staged between October and June. In July and August, performances move outside, with a stage backed by the ruins of the Baths of Caracalla – a fantastic setting. (www.operaroma.it)

Shopping

LOL

CLOTHING

20 MAP P122, B5

Fabio Casentini's beautifully curated collection of women's clothing, with chalky, muted colours and delicate fabrics. There is some

Teatro dell'Opera di Roma

lovely and well-priced jewelry as well. (http://lolroma.com)

Perlei
JEWELLERY

21 MAP P122, A4

This tiny artisanal jeweller on Monti's best shopping street showcases handmade pieces by Tammar Edelman and Elinor Avni that will appeal to those with a modernist aesthetic – the graceful arcs, sinuous strands and architectural arrangements are elegant and eye-catching. (www.perlei.com)

Tina Sondergaard
FASHION & ACCESSORIES

22 MAP P122, A4

With a Scandi, retro look, superbly cut, Tina Sondergaard's beautifully handmade creations for women are a unique buy; you can have adjustments made (included in the price). (www.tinasondergaard.com)

Pifebo
VINTAGE

23 MAP P122, A5

Seek out a secondhand steal at Pifebo, the city's top vintage boutique. Shelves and racks brim with sunglasses, boots, clothing (including lots of denim), bags and an impressive sports jersey collection, all hailing from the '70s, '80s and '90s. The shop also specialises in rehabbing and restoring leather items, handily returning them to their original splendour. (www.pifebo.com)

Walking Tour 🚶

Hanging Out in San Lorenzo

San Lorenzo is a gritty, historically working-class district, but scratch beneath the graffiti-coated surface and this is one of Rome's most creative neighbourhoods, dotted with small galleries and studios. Its proximity to the huge Sapienza University, founded in 1303, gives the area a buzz, especially on summer evenings.

Getting There

🚶 It's about 1km walk from Termini station.

🚋 Catch tram 19 or 3.

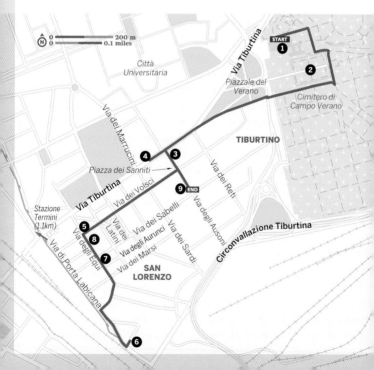

❶ Basilica di San Lorenzo Fuori le Mura

Standing on the site of St Lawrence's burial place, this **basilica** is one of Rome's four papal basilicas. It suffered bomb damage in WWII and was subsequently carefully rebuilt. It retains a stunning Cosmati floor and a 13th-century frescoed portico.

❷ Cimitero di Campo Verano

The **Cimitero di Campo Verano** (www.cimitericapitolini.it) dates to the Napoleonic occupation of Rome (1804–14), when the French decreed burials should take place outside the city walls. Famous (non)-residents include novelist Alberto Moravia, politician Andreotti, the actor Marcello Mastroianni and the director Roberto Rossellini.

❸ Fondazione Pastificio Cerere

This sometime **pasta factory** (www.pastificiocerere.it), abandoned in the 1970s, now houses artists' studios and has regular exhibitions, curated in association with organisations such as the British School. It's the beating heart of the San Lorenzo fine art scene.

❹ Chocolate Stop

It's time to delve into San Lorenzo's dining scene. Start at **Said** (www.said.it), a boutique cafe-restaurant in a converted 1920s factory. The menu is chocolate-centred, including even some of the savoury dishes, such as beef with chocolate sauce (rather like a Mexican mole).

❺ Laboratorio Pellerossa

Once sated, it's time to shop. **Laboratorio Pellerossa** is an old-fashioned leather and metalwork workshop, crammed from floor to ceiling with belts and bags. You can buy handmade accessories or get something fixed, as well as buy inexpensive metalwork jewellery.

❻ Terzo Fronte

Peruse contemporary **Terzo Fronte**, the brainchild of French expats, curator Georgia René-Worms and film-maker Colin Ledoux, who live on site. Exhibitions take over their entire living space, making for an always interesting dynamic.

❼ Craft Beer

If you're ready to savour the drinking scene, the friendly bar staff at **Artisan** (www.facebook.com/art.isan.90) are always happy to recommend particular craft beers from its large range. There is also a selection of tasty snacks.

❽ Eat with the Beats

With mismatched vintage furniture and a boho feel, **Officine Beat** (https://officinebeat.it) offers a good range of cocktails and food, including an excellent *cacio e pepe* (classic Roman cheese and pepper pasta).

❾ Last Orders

Close your day at local favourite **Bar Celestino** (www.facebook.com/bar-celestino). Fight your way through the crowd and claim a seat inside or join the grungy regulars drinking on the pavement.

Explore ⊕
San Giovanni
& Celio

Southeast of the city centre, the Basilica di San Giovanni in Laterano is Rome's cathedral. It's the focus of an area that is otherwise mainly residential 19th-century housing blocks. Nearby, the Celio (Caelian), one of Rome's seven hills, rises south of the Colosseum, and harbours beautiful medieval churches, the extraordinary subterranean Basilica of San Clemente, a pocket-sized gay area, and lovely Villa Celimontana park.

The Short List

○ **Basilica di San Giovanni in Laterano (p134)** Exploring the splendours of Rome's cathedral, one of the city's four patriarchal basilicas.

○ **Basilica di San Clemente (p137)** Going deep underground at this multilayered church, reaching a Mithraic altar beneath.

○ **Chiesa di Santo Stefano Rotondo (p137)** Feeling the atmosphere of this haunting ancient church, with its gore-packed frescoes.

Getting There & Around

🚌 Buses 85 and 714 serve San Giovanni from Termini. Bus 87 stops in San Giovanni en route to/from the centro storico.

Ⓜ Lines A and C serve San Giovanni.

🚋 No 3 goes to Testaccio and on to Trastevere.

Neighbourhood Map on p136

Chiesa di Santo Stefano Rotondo REPORT/SHUTTERSTOCK ©

Top Experience 📷

Explore the Basilica di San Giovanni in Laterano

⊙ MAP P136, E3

This monumental church, the oldest of the city's four papal basilicas, is Rome's official cathedral and the pope's seat as the Bishop of Rome. Dating from the 4th century, it's revered as the mater et caput (mother and head) of all Catholic churches and was the pope's main place of worship for almost a thousand years.

The Facade

Crowned by fifteen 7m-high statues – Christ, with St John the Baptist, John the Evangelist and the twelve Apostles – Alessandro Galilei's immense late-baroque facade was added in 1735. In the portico behind the colossal columns, look out for the **central bronze doors,** which were moved here from the Curia in the Roman Forum, and, on the far right, the **Holy Door**, which is only opened in Jubilee years.

The Interior

The first impression on entering the church is one of vastness: this is a space that makes you feel small. Above, the coffered gilt **ceiling** dates to the 16th century, while the Cosimati floor is 15th century **mosaic**. Baroque genius Borromini was asked to restore the church for the 1650 Jubilee, but to redesign while retaining its older elements. The sweeping **central nave** is lined with 18th-century sculptures of the apostles, each 4.6m high and set in its own dramatic niche.

At the head of the nave, an elaborate Gothic **baldachin** towers over the papal altar. Dating to the 14th century, this is said to contain the relics of the heads of saints Peter and Paul. In front of it, at the base of the altar, the tomb of Pope Martin V lies in the **confessio** along with a wooden statue of St John the Baptist.

The massive **apse** is decorated with sparkling mosaics, some of which survive from the original 4th-century basilica. Most, however, were added in the 1800s. At the other end of the basilica, you'll find an incomplete **Giotto fresco** on the first pillar in the right-hand nave.

The Cloister

The basilica's 13th-century cloister is an oasis of peace. Set around a central garden, its ambulatories are lined with graceful twisted columns and marble fragments from the original church, including the remains of a 5th-century papal throne and inscriptions of two papal bulls.

★ **Top Tips**

○ Make sure to look down as well as up – the inlaid mosaic floor is a wonderful work of art in its own right.

○ In the cloister, look out for a slab of porphyry on which it's said Roman soldiers threw lots to win the robe of the crucified Christ.

○ Check out the Giotto fresco on the first column in the right-hand aisle.

○ There's an information office to the right of the portico, as well as inside, where you can buy tickets for the cloister and rent audioguides.

✕ **Take a Break**

For lunch you're best off heading downhill towards the Colosseum, where you can lunch on classic trattoria food at Il Bocconcino (p140) or tasty cafe fare at Cafè Cafè (p139). For dinner, head farther into San Giovanni to splendid local favourite Santopalato.

San Giovanni & Celio

A | B | C | D | E | F

1 | 2 | 3 | 4

N

200 m
0.1 miles

Via di Quintino

Via Statilla

Manzoni Ⓜ

Via Emanuele Filiberto

Via Tasso

Santuario della Scala

Santa & Sancta
Sanctorum

**SAN
GIOVANNI**

Via Boiardo

Ⓜ San Giovanni

Piazzale
San Giovanni

Via Magna Grecia Ⓜ

8 ✕ Via Velo

Via Sannio

Piazzale
Appio

Via di Porta
San Giovanni

7 ⊙ Piazza di Porta
San Giovanni

Via Amiterno

Via Merulana

Via Galilei

Via Ariosto

Via Merulana

6 ⊙ Obelisk
Piazza di
San Giovanni
in Laterano

**Basilica di
San Giovanni
in Laterano**

Viale Manzoni

Via Ruggero Bonghi

Via P Villari

Via di San Giovanni in Laterano

Via dell'Amba Aradam

Via Ferretella in Laterano

Via Ipponio

Via Poliziano

Via Iside

Piazza
Iside

18 ⊙

Basilica dei
SS Quattro
Coronati

Via di Santi Quattro

Via de Ferretella in Laterano

17 ✕

Via Merulana

Via Crescimbeni

Via Muratori

1 ⊙ Basilica di
San Clemente

3 ⊙

CELIO

Via di Santo Stefano Rotondo

2 ⊙ Chiesa di Santo
Stefano Rotondo

Via di Sant'Erasmo

Piazza Porta
Metronia

Via Labicana

Via Mecenate

Via N Salvi

Via della Domus Aurea

Parco del Colle Oppio

11 ⊙

Via di Querceti

Via Celimontana

Via della Navicella

Piazza del
Colosseo

My
Bar
🟤
Coming Out

10 ✕
16 ✕
13 ✕
9 ✕ ✕ 15
12 ✕
14 ✕

Via Capo
d'Africa

Via M
Aurelio

Via Ostilia

Via Annia

Via Claudia

Via della Croce

Colosseo Ⓜ

Parco del Celio

Viale del Parco del Celio

Clivo di S Scauro

Via di Celio Vibenna

5 ⊙ Case
Romane

4 ⊙ Villa
Celimontana

For reviews see	
⊙ Top Experiences	p134
⊙ Sights	p137
✕ Eating	p139
✕ Drinking	p141
🅐 Shopping	p141

Sights

Basilica di San Clemente

BASILICA

1 🎯 MAP P136, C2

Nowhere illustrates the many levels of Rome's history better than this multileveled church. The ground-level 12th-century basilica sits atop a 4th-century church, which, in turn, stands over a 2nd-century pagan temple and a 1st-century Roman house. Beneath everything are foundations dating from the Roman Republic, and you can hear the rush of an underground spring through a grill in the floor. Tickets can only be booked online. (www. basilicasanclemente.com)

Chiesa di Santo Stefano Rotondo

CHURCH

2 🎯 MAP P136, C3

Set in its own secluded grounds, this church dates from the 5th century and is the Hungarian national church in Rome. It feels more like a temple than a church, with an unusual, circular interior and inner colonnade. On the walls is a cycle of 16th-century frescoes graphically depicting the tortures suffered by many early Christian martyrs.

Basilica dei SS Quattro Coronati

BASILICA

3 🎯 MAP P136, C2

This brooding fortified church harbours some lovely 13th-

Basilica di San Clemente

SIR FRANCIS CANKER PHOTOGRAPHY/GETTY IMAGES ©

century frescoes and a delightful hidden cloister, accessible from the left-hand aisle. The frescoes, in the **Oratorio di San Silvestro**, depict the story of Constantine and Pope Sylvester I and the so-called Donation of Constantine, a notorious forged document with which the emperor supposedly ceded control of Rome and the Western Roman Empire to the papacy. To access the Oratorio, ring the bell in the second courtyard. (www.monacheagostiniane antiquattrocoronati.it)

Villa Celimontana PARK

4 ◎ MAP P136, B4

With its grassy banks and colourful flower beds, this leafy park is a wonderful place to escape the crowds and enjoy a summer picnic. At its centre is a 16th-century villa housing the Italian Geographical Society, while to the south stands a 12m-plus Egyptian obelisk. In July, it's the setting for a much-loved summer jazz festival.

Case Romane CHRISTIAN SITE

5 ◎ MAP P136, A3

According to tradition, two Roman soldiers, John and Paul (not to be confused with the Apostles), lived in these houses before they were beheaded by the emperor Julian. There's no direct evidence for this, although research has revealed that the houses were

used for Christian worship. This is an extraordinary underground site, where many of the around 20 rooms have retained their rich decoration. There are regular evening tours and wine tastings here in summer; check the website. (www. coopculture.it)

Obelisk MONUMENT

6 ◎ MAP P136, E3

Overlooking Palazzo Laterano, this is said to be the world's largest standing Egyptian obelisk. Topping off at almost 46m, it's also the oldest of Rome's 13 ancient obelisks, dating from the 15th century BCE. It originally stood in a temple in Thebes but was shipped to Rome by Constantine II and, after various relocations, placed in its current position in 1588.

Santuario della Scala Santa & Sancta Sanctorum CHRISTIAN SITE

7 ◎ MAP P136, E3

The Scala Santa, said to be the staircase Jesus walked up in Pontius Pilate's palace in Jerusalem, was brought to Rome by St Helena in the 4th century. Pilgrims consider it sacred and climb it on their knees, saying a prayer on each of the 28 steps. At the top, behind an iron grating, is the richly decorated Sancta Sanctorum (Holy of Holies), formerly the pope's private chapel. (www.scala-santa.it)

Church of Horrors

Santo Stefano Rotondo is decorated by a series of gruesome frescoes, so gory that even the Marquis de Sade was disgusted. Charles Dickens likened seeing them to a fever dream; 'To single out details from the great dream of Roman Churches, would be the wildest occupation in the world. But St. Stefano Rotondo, a damp, mildewed vault of an old church in the outskirts of Rome, will always struggle uppermost in my mind, by reason of the hideous paintings with which its walls are covered. Such a panorama of horror and butchery no man could imagine in his sleep, though he were to eat a whole pig raw, for supper.'

What possessed the artist, Niccolò Circignani, to depict the torments undergone by each martyr? The paintings were commissioned during the religious struggles of the 16th century, at the height of the Counter Reformation, when the Catholic church was attempting to stem the tide of Protestantism. The images would have underlined the suffering the early Christians had endured in order to establish their true church, and, perhaps, would inspire and chasten new generations of devout (and terrified) Catholics.

Eating

Santo Palato
ITALIAN

8 MAP P136, F4

The name means 'Holy Palate', an indication of quite how seriously female chef Sarah Cicolini takes her dedication to cooking perfect versions of Roman classics, such as *cacio e pepe* (cheese and pepper) and carbonara (with *guanciale* and egg) in this renowned Roman neighbourhood restaurant. (http://santopalato.superbexperience.com)

Aroma
GASTRONOMY €€€

9 MAP P136, B1

For the ultimate meal-with-a-view, the rooftop restaurant of luxury Palazzo Manfredi hotel offers peerless panoramas over the Colosseum, and Michelin-starred food to boot. Overseeing the kitchen is chef Giuseppe Di Iorio, whose seasonal menus reflect his passion for inventive, forward-thinking Mediterranean cuisine. A gluten-free tasting menu is available and there's a less formal bistro next door. (www.aromarestaurant.it)

Cafè Cafè

BISTRO €

10 ✖ MAP P136, B2

This cramped and welcoming cafe-bistro is a far cry from the many impersonal eateries around the Colosseum. With its rustic wooden tables, butternut walls and wine bottles, it's a charming spot for a breakfast pancake, lunch salad or afternoon tea and cake. It also does takeaway panini, ideal for a picnic in Villa Celimontana. (www.cafecafebistrot.it)

Li Rioni

PIZZA €

11 ✖ MAP P136, C2

This bustling joint serves the best pizza in the Celio neighbourhood, an easy walk from the Colosseum. Locals and tourists squeeze into the noisy interior – set up as a Roman street scene – and tuck into crispy fried starters and bubbling wood-charred pizzas in the thin-crust Roman style. (www.lirioni.it)

Divin Ostilia

ITALIAN €€

12 ✖ MAP P136, B1

A popular choice near the Colosseum, Divin Ostilia is everything you want in a wine bar: conviviality, bottle-lined walls, high ceilings and feasts of cheese and cured meats, classic pastas and grilled steaks on which to graze alongside a fine range of Italian wines.

View of the Colosseum from Aroma (p139)

Il Bocconcino

LAZIO €€

13 MAP P136, B2

One of the better options in the touristy pocket near the Colosseum, this easy-going trattoria stands out for its authentic regional cooking. Daily specials are chalked up on blackboards or there's a regular menu of classic Roman pastas, grilled meats and imaginative desserts. (www.ilbocconcino.com)

Taverna dei Quaranta

ROMAN €€

14 MAP P136

Tasty traditional food and a prime location – near the Colosseum but just off the beaten track – are the hallmarks of this family-run trattoria. It serves traditional dishes, in large portions, and feels refreshingly authentic in this touristy 'hood. (www.tavernadeiquaranta.com)

Drinking

Court

COCKTAIL BAR

15 MAP P136, B1

In the courtyard of Palazzo Manfredi, this 'smart casual' super-chic cocktail bar overseen by Matteo Zed has views over the former gladiator school, and to the Colosseum beyond. Cocktail creations include Spicy Paloma, a zingy Patron Silver, Amaro, lime and grapefruit creation, and an Old-Fashioned with added truffle. (www.aromarestaurant.it)

Wine Concept

WINE BAR

16 MAP P136, B2

This white-walled, contemporary-feeling *enoteca* (wine bar) is staffed by expert sommeliers and has an extensive list of Italian regional labels, natural organic wines and European vintages, as well as a limited food menu. Wines are available to drink by the glass or to buy by the bottle, and there are also daily tastings (you can try three wines plus aperitivo snacks). (www.wineconcept.it)

Shopping

Pifebo

VINTAGE

17 MAP P136, C4

One of Rome's best-stocked secondhand and vintage clothes stores. There are rich pickings among the racks of leather jackets, denims, sunglasses and cowboy boots. (www.pifebo.com)

Soul Food

MUSIC

18 MAP P136, D2

Run by Hate Records, Soul Food is a laid-back record store with an encyclopaedic collection of vinyl that runs the musical gamut from '60s garage and rockabilly to punk, indie, new wave, folk, funk and soul. You'll also find retro T-shirts, posters, fanzines and even vintage toys. (www.haterecords.com)

Explore ◈

Aventino & Testaccio

The Aventino (Aventine Hill) is a wisteria-laden idyll of residential villas, gardens and churches, set above the hulking ruins of the Caracalla Roman Baths. At the base of the hill, the former working-class district of Testaccio is the heart (liver and lungs) of Rome's offal-based cuisine, and feels like a small town within the city.

The Short List

o **Terme di Caracalla (p147)** *Wandering the colossal remains of this bath complex, with barely another tourist in sight.*

o **Basilica di Santa Sabina (p148)** *This ancient church stands on a hilltop alongside the lovely orange tree garden of Parco Savello.*

o **Villa del Priorato di Malta (p148)** *Looking through a keyhole for a whimsically brilliant view of St Peter's dome.*

o **Cimitero Acattolico per gli Stranieri (p147)** *Seeking out poets Keats and Shelley in the world's most romantic cemetery.*

Getting There & Around

🚌 Bus 714 for the Terme di Caracalla.

Ⓜ For Testaccio, take line B to Piramide. The Aventino is walkable from Testaccio, or from Circo Massimo (line B).

🚋 From San Giovanni, tram 3 runs along Viale Aventino, through Testaccio and on to Trastevere.

Neighbourhood Map on p146

Terme di Caracalla MISTERVLAD/SHUTTERSTOCK ©

Walking Tour 🥾

A Taste of Testaccio

A grid of stolid 19th-century housing blocks, Testaccio grew up as a working-class neighbourhood centred on Rome's slaughterhouse. It is now famous for being the epicentre of true Roman cuisine, its historic food market, its romantic cemetery and its distinct local character. It offers a glimpse of neighbourhood Rome, with the sense of a small town within a town.

Walk Facts

Start Cimitero Acattolico per gli Stranieri; metro Piramide

End Piazza Testaccio; metro Piramide

Length 2.5km; up to six hours

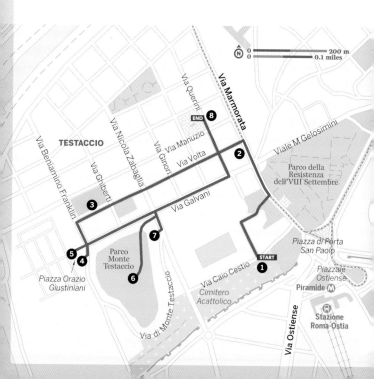

❶ The World's Most Romantic Cemetery

Rome's **Cimitero Acattolico per gli Stranieri** (p147), or 'non-Catholic' cemetery, has a palpable air of Grand Tour romance and tragedy. This beautiful site is where romantic poets Keats and Shelley are buried, having died in Italy. Writer Johann Goethe and Italian thinker Antonio Gramsci are also buried here, while the most spectacular of the graves is an ancient Roman pyramid, commissioned by an Egyptophile general.

❷ Pasticceria Barberini

Having indulged in some elegaic melancholy courtesy of the cemetery, head for an uplifting coffee and *cornetto* (croissant filled with jam, cream or chocolate) at **Pasticceria Barberini** (www.pasticceriabarberini.it).

❸ Market Meanderings

Testaccio's neighbourhood market, the **Nuovo Mercato di Testaccio** (p103), is a glorious place, where you can buy delicious produce and products, and there are some glorious places to pick up a snack, including gourmet slices of pizza at **Casamanco** and sandwiches filled with traditional Roman offal turned into meltingly good stews at **Mordi e Vai** (p150).

❹ Atmospheric Coffee Hit

The tiny kiosk, **Bar Tabacchi da Rosa e Andrea**, outside a former abattoir, feels unchanged since its incarnation in the 1950s. Rosa serves up lightning bolt shots of espresso.

❺ The Mattatoio

Admire art at the **Mattatoio** (www.mattatoioroma.it), one of Rome's top contemporary arts venues. The 19th-century complex was the city's main abattoir until 1975, and later became one of the city's most famous squatted arts centres.

❻ Monte Testaccio

The Roman hillock of **Monte Testaccio** is actually an ancient rubbish dump. This 54m-high grass-capped mound is a huge pile of amphorae fragments (*testae* in Latin), dating to the time when Testaccio was ancient Rome's river port.

❼ Flavio al Velavevodetto

Sample authentic *cucina romana* (Roman cuisine) at **Flavio al Velavevodetto** (www.ristorantevelavevodetto.it). Dishes may include, season permitting, *carciofo alla giudia* (deep-fried artichoke) and superlative *rigatoni alla carbonara* (pasta tubes wrapped in a silky egg sauce spiked with morsels of cured pig's cheek), but the *cacio e pepe* is of particular renown.

❽ L'Oasi della Birra

On Testaccio's main piazza, the long-running **L'Oasi della Birra** (p150) has a sweeping menu of international beers and some superlative cold cuts and cheeses to go along with them. Bag a place at one of the long tables on the terrace for a view on the comings and goings of the square.

Aventino & Testaccio

Sights ⊙
Eating ⊗
Drinking ⊙
Shopping ⊕

CELIO

Viale delle Terme di Caracalla

Via di Valle delle Camene

Via Antonina

1 ⊙ Terme di Caracalla

Viale Guido Baccelli

Via di Villa Pepoli

Viale delle Terme di Caracalla

Via dei Cerchi

Viale Guido Baccelli

Via del Circo Massimo

Circo Massimo

Viale Aventino

Via Aventina

Via Peruzzi

Piazza Gian Lorenzo Bernini

Viale Giotto

Via di Porta Ardeatina

Via Odoardo Beccari

Viale Marco Polo

Piazzale Ugo La Malta

Via Terme Deciane

Roseto Comunale

Via di Prisca

11 ⊙
Via di San Saba

Viale della Piramide Cestia

Via Anna Faustina

Giardino degli Aranci

5 ⊙

Basilica di Santa Sabina

4 ⊙ 3 ⊙

Villa del Priorato di Malta

Via di Santa Sabina

AVENTINO

Piazza Santa Prisca

Clivo de Publici

Via San Domenica

Via di San Alessio

Piazza Albania

Via Melania

Via M Gelsomini

Piazza della Piramide di Caio Cestio

Piramide di Caio Cestio

Piramide

Stazione Roma-Ostia

Via Ostiense

Via dei Conciatori

Porta di Ripa Grande

Via di San Michele

Ponte Sublicio

Piazzale Portuense

Lgt Testaccio

Via Cecchi

Via Gessi

Via Vanvitelli

7 ⊗

Piazza Santa Maria Liberatrice

Via Giovanni Battista Bodini

2 ⊗

Piazza Testaccio

15 ⊙
9 ⊗
8 ⊗

Via Marmorata

Via Ginori

Via Galvani

13 ⊙

TESTACCIO

Via Branca

Via Florio

6 ⊗

10 ⊗

Via Nicola Zabaglia

Via Volta

Via Beniamino Franklin

Cimitero Acattolico per gli Stranieri

Via Caio Cestio

Ponte Testaccio

Viale del Campo Boario

Parco Monte Testaccio

Largo Dino Frisullo

Via di Monte Testaccio

14 ⊙

Piazza Orazio Giustiniani

Lgt Testaccio

Via Portuense

Viale di Trastevere

Tiber River

200 m
0.1 miles

Sights

Terme di Caracalla
RUINS

1 ⊙ MAP P146, F3

The emperor Caracalla had this vast baths complex inaugurated in 212 CE. It spread across 10 hectares, comprising baths, gyms, libraries, shops and gardens, and was used by up to 8000 people daily. The ruins are still vast, impressive, with few visitors, and to see how they once would have been, you can hire a virtual reality headset from the ticket office. The focal point is the central **bathhouse**, a huge rectangular edifice bookended by two **palestre** (gyms). (www.coopculture.it)

Cimitero Acattolico per gli Stranieri
CEMETERY

2 ⊙ MAP P146, C4

Rome's Cimitero Acattolico per gli Stranieri, or 'non-Catholic' cemetery, has a palpable air of Grand Tour romance and tragedy. This beautiful site is where romantic poets Keats and Shelley are buried, having died in Italy respectively of consumption and drowning, as well as the poet Johann Goethe and Italian political thinker Antonio Gramsci. Among the gravestones and cypress trees, look out for the *Angelo del Dolore* (Angel of Grief), a much-replicated 1894 sculpture that US artist William Wetmore Story created for his wife's grave. (www.cemeteryrome.it)

Cimitero Acattolico per gli Stranieri

DMYTRO SURKOV/SHUTTERSTOCK ©

Giardino degli Aranci

Villa del Priorato di Malta

HISTORIC BUILDING

3 MAP P146, C1

Fronting a cypress-shaded piazza that was designed by Piranesi, the Roman headquarters of the Sovereign Order of Malta (aka the Cavalieri di Malta, or Knights of Malta) provides Rome's most extraordinary view.

It's not immediately apparent, but look through the keyhole in the villa's green door and you'll see the dome of St Peter's Basilica perfectly aligned at the end of a hedge-lined avenue.

Basilica di Santa Sabina

BASILICA

4 MAP P146, C1

This solemn basilica, one of Rome's most beautiful early Christian churches, was founded by Peter of Illyria around 422 CE. It was enlarged in the 9th century and again in 1216, just before it was given to the newly founded Dominican order – note the tombstone of Muñoz de Zamora, one of the order's founding fathers, in the nave floor. The interior was further modified by Domenico Fontana in 1587. A 20th-century restoration subsequently returned it to its original look.

Giardino degli Aranci
PARK

5 MAP P146, C1

Officially called the Parco Savello but known to every Roman as the *Giardino degli Aranci* (Orange Garden), this walled park is a hidden-feeling romantic haven. Head down the central avenue, passing towering umbrella pines and lawns planted with blooming orange trees, to bask in heavenly views across Rome's rooftops to the dome of St Peter's.

Eating

Trapizzino
FAST FOOD €

6 ✖ MAP P146, B3

The original of a growing country-wide chain, this is the birthplace of the *trapizzino,* a kind of hybrid sandwich made by stuffing a cone of doughy focaccia with fillers such as *polpette al sugo* (meatballs in tomato sauce) or *pollo alla cacciatore* (stewed chicken). They're messy to eat but quite delicious. Eat in or take away; beer and wine available. (www.trapizzino.it)

Pizzeria Da Remo
PIZZA €

7 ✖ MAP P146, B2

This is the ultimate Roman pizza experience. Join the queue to dine with cheerful crowds here at one of the city's best-known and most popular pizzerias. It's all about the no-frills decor, the brusque waiters, the superlative *fritti* (fried things, such as zucchini flower), and crispy wafer-thin pizzas, loaded with delicious overspilling toppings.

Felice a Testaccio
TRATTORIA €€

8 ✖ MAP P146, B3

This neighbourhood trattoria is renowned for its unswerving dedication to Roman soul food. Though its decor is contemporary, the menu is unrelentingly old school, including dishes such as filled ravioli, fried *baccalà* (cod), *involtino* (beef rolls in a tomato sauce) and *saltimbocca* (veal escalopes with proscuitto and sage). Vegetable sides include seasonal delights such as artichokes, asparagus and *puntarelle* (a type of chicory). (www.feliceatestaccio.it)

The Fifth Quarter

The Roman love of nose-to-tail eating arose in Testaccio around the city abattoir, when workers' pay was topped up with the cheapest cuts of meat. This is thus the centre of this most Roman of cuisines, and neighbourhood trattorias serve traditional offal-based dishes. So whether you want to avoid them or give them a go, look out for *pajata* (veal intestines), *trippa* (tripe), *coratella* (heart, lung and liver), *animelle* (sweetbreads), along with *coda alla vaccinara* (oxtail), *testarella* (head), *lingua* (tongue) and *zampe* (trotters).

Taverna Volpetti
ITALIAN €€

9 MAP P146, C3

An offshoot of the famous Volpetti deli (p151), this casual restaurant serves a cosmopolitan menu of beloved Roman pastas and creative modern mains. However, its forte is its selection of cured meats and cheeses, served on platters showcasing fine Parma prosciutto, Alpine *formaggio* and prized Iberian hams. (www.tavernavolpetti.it)

Mordi e Vai
STREET FOOD €

10 MAP P146, B3

Come at lunchtime and you'll have to elbow your way through the crowds at Sergio Esposito's critically acclaimed market stall, which serves up panini filled with classic Roman dishes, such as the signature *panino con l'allesso di scottona* (bread roll filled with meltingly tender slow-cooked beef). (www.mordievai.it)

Al Fresco
Opera

The hulking ruins of the vast 3rd-century **Terme di Caracalla** (www.operaroma.it) set the memorable stage for the Teatro dell'Opera's summer season of music and ballet, with performances by big-name Italian and international artists.

Marco Martini Restaurant
GASTRONOMY €€€

11 MAP P146, D2

In a leafy indoor garden with tiled floors, this exceptional restaurant under chef Marco Martini at the Corner Townhouse offers informal fine-dining on Aventino Hill. The man with his name on the menu is one of Rome's youngest Michelin-starred chefs, whose inventive dishes often riff on Italian culinary traditions. Order à la carte or opt for one of several tasting menus, including one for vegetarians. (www.marcomartinichef.com)

Drinking

L'Oasi della Birra
CRAFT BEER

12 MAP P146, B3

Housed in the Palombi Enoteca bottle shop, L'Oasi della Birra is exactly that – an oasis of beer. Offering hundreds of labels – everything from German heavyweights to British bitters – as well as wines, cheeses and cold cuts, it's deservedly popular. Sit in the cramped cellar or on the piazza-side terrace at long tables that encourage conviviality. (www.facebook.com/EnotecaPalombi1917)

Tram Depot
BAR

13 MAP P146, C3

When temperatures climb in the capital, this charming little kiosk-bar springs to life until late into the night, serving up coffee, excellent *cornetti* (croissants),

Volpetti

grattacecca (crushed ice with fruit) and cocktails. Its outdoor seating, vintage porch swings, fairy lights, grass-style flooring and setting flanked by trees conjure up a garden-party vibe. (www.facebook.com/tramdepotroma)

Ch 18 87
COCKTAIL BAR

14 MAP P146, B4

Hidden away on the low-ceilinged first floor above the historic restaurant Checchino Dal 1887, this bar feels like a local secret, and takes its cocktails seriously, with head bartender Simone Mina creating exquisite tipples, some of which match with certain snacks, such as 'Deep Honey' (a blend of

cachaça, tarocco, caradache, bitters and vermouth), paired with a half-portion of cacio e pepe.

Shopping

Volpetti
FOOD & DRINKS

15 MAP P146, C3

Begun by two Umbrian brothers in the 1960s, this is no longer run by the same family, but remains a treasure trove of gourmet delicacies. Helpful staff will guide you through the extensive selection of Italian cheese, homemade pasta, olive oil, vinegar, cured meat, wine and grappa. It also serves excellent, though pricey, sliced pizza. (www.volpetti.com)

Walking Tour

Ostiense & San Paolo

Gritty, post-industrial Ostiense houses a buzzy university campus and is a local favourite for its worth-a-trip bars and restaurants and Rome's branch of Eataly. There's also street art, a power station turned classical art museum, after-hours hedonism in former factories and the world's third-largest church.

Getting There

M Line B runs to Piramide, Garbatella and Basilica San Paolo.

Routes 23, 769 and 792 serve Via Ostiense.

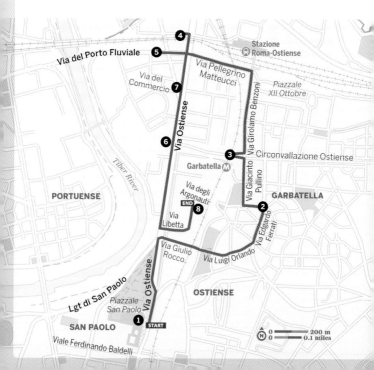

1 St Paul's
Magnificent Basilica

Basilica di San Paolo Fuori le Mura
(www.basilicasanpaolo.org) is one of
Rome's four papal churches and is
an impressive sight, despite having
been largely destroyed by fire in 1823.
It was subsequently rebuilt, integrat-
ing some of the surving features,
including the 5th-century triumphal
arch and Gothic tabernacle.

2 Garbatella

Garbatella was founded in 1920
as a garden suburb for workers,
which Mussolini then used to
resettle residents displaced by his
destruction of neighbourhoods in
the city centre. It's a unique area
in Rome, where art deco villas
have their own gardens. There's
a popular flea market here, and
you can stop for a glass of natural
wine at lovely **La Mescita** (www.
enotecalamescita.it), overlooked
by the area's art deco **Teatro
Palladium** (http://teatropalladium.
uniroma3.it).

3 A View on the Bridge

As you walk towards the next
stop, get a view across to **Ponte
Settimia Spizzichino**. This bridge
was designed by Francesco del To-
sto, and is named after one of the
sole Roman Jewish survivors of
the Holocaust. The white-coated,
graceful feat of engineering links
Via Ostiense to Garbatella, the
neighbourhood where Spizzichino
lived until her death in 2000.

4 Trattoria Pennestri

For lunch, if you're here on the weekend (otherwise it's open evenings),
eat at **Trattoria Pennestri** (http://
trattoriapennestri.it), a contemporary
take on the trattoria with Roman
classics cooked with finesse. If it's
a weekday, push on to **Eataly** (www.
eataly.net), a vast foodie complex with
nearly 20 restaurants and cafes.

5 Street Art

Stroll down **Via del Porto Fluviale**
to see some of Rome's most
inventive street murals. Standouts
include works by BLU, an Italian
artist, where the windows of a
former aeronautical building have
been turned into monsters' eyes.

6 Centrale Montemartini

In an ex-powerplant, ancient
sculpture is juxtaposed against
engines and furnaces at
Centrale Montemartini (www.
centralemontemartini.org), an outpost
of the Capitoline Museums.

7 Doppiozeroo

You'll need to retrace your steps a little to **Doppiozeroo** (www.doppiozeroo.
com), where urbane Romans flock
from around 6pm to 9pm for its
meal-worthy *aperitivo* buffet (waiters
will bring a selection to your table).

8 Beat Drop

To get your groove on, head to
warehouse-club **Circolo Degli Il-
luminati** (www.circolodegliilluminati.
it;), getting the party going with a
hectic array of international DJs
and live sets.

Worth a Trip 👀
Tour the Via Appia Antica

Via Appia Antica is an ancient Roman road running southwards out of the city, built to enable the swift movement of Roman troops. It feels like a rural escape, and the beautiful cobbled, pine-lined thoroughfare is a glorious place for a walk or a cycle, with some evocative ruins along the way.

www.parcoappiaantica.it

Chiesa del Domine Quo Vadis

This pint-sized church marks the spot where St Peter, fleeing Rome, met a vision of Jesus going the other way. When Peter asked, 'Domine, quo vadis?' (Lord, where are you going?), Jesus replied, 'Venio Roman iterum crucifigi,' (I am coming to Rome to be crucified again). Reluctantly deciding to join him, Peter tramped back into town where he was arrested and executed.

Catacombe di San Callisto

Founded in the 2nd century, this is Rome's largest network of **catacombs** (www.catacombe.roma.it) extending for more than 20km in a tangle of tunnels. Visits are by tour, to a section of the network, with a selection of tombs that includes 16 popes, scores of martyrs and thousands of Christians.

Catacombe di Santa Domitilla

Set a little way away from the cluster of main sights, these **catacombs** (www.domitilla.info) feature the underground **Chiesa di SS Nereus e Achilleus**, a 4th-century church dedicated to two Roman soldiers martyred by Diocletian.

On a tour, you'll see the church, some exquisite Christian wall art and just a fraction of the tunnels, which extend roughly 17km.

Basilica & Catacombe di San Sebastiano

One of the two main Appian Way catacombs, this complex contains frescoes, stucco work, epigraphs and several immaculately preserved mausoleums. The catacombs extend for more than 12km and once harboured more than 65,000 tombs.

The original 4th-century **basilica** (www.sansebastianofuorilemura.org) was mostly destroyed in the 9th century and the church you see today dates mainly from the 17th century. It is dedicated to St Sebastian, who was martyred and buried here in the late 3rd century. In the **Capella delle**

★ Top Tips

○ Bikes and e-bikes are available to rent at the helpful **Appia Antica Regional Park Information Centre** (www.parcoappiaantica.it), which also has maps.

○ The information centre is at the northern starting point of the road, close to the 118 bus stop.

✕ Take a Break

Enjoy a garden lunch at **Il Giardino di Giulia e Fratelli** (www.facebook.com/ilgiardinodigiuliaefratelli), a friendly, family-run, bucolic garden restaurant, near the Mausoleo di Cecilia Metella. Local families come here for leisurely lunches.

★ Getting There

Metro & Bus Bus 118 stops at Circus Massimus, Piazza Venezia and Colosseum before going on to Appia Antica. Or take line A to Colli-Albani Metro, then bus 664.

Reliquie you'll find an arrow used to kill him and the column to which he was tied.

A warren of tunnels that lie beneath the church, the **Catacombe di San Sebastiano** (www.catacombe.org) were the first catacombs to be so called, the name deriving from the Greek *kata* (near) and *kymbas* (cavity), because they were located near a cave. During the persecution of Christians by the emperor Vespasian from 258 CE, some believe that the catacombs were used as a safe haven for the remains of St Peter and St Paul.

Villa di Massenzio

Maxentius' huge 4th-century palace complex includes the **Circo di Massenzio** (www.villadimassenzio.it), Rome's best-preserved ancient racetrack. The 10,000-seat arena was built by Maxentius around 309, but he died before ever seeing a race here.

Overlooking the vast site, the namesake **Villa di Massenzio** (www.villadimassenzio.it) itself is closed for long-term archaeological investigations.

Mausoleo di Cecilia Metella

This barrel-shaped **mausoleum** (www.coopculture.it) from the 1st century BCE encloses a now roofless burial chamber. It was built for Quintus Metellus Creticus's daughter, who was of particular significance, as she joined two important families by marriage. In the 14th century it was converted into a fort by the Caetani family and used to collect tolls from passing traffic.

Villa dei Quintili

This 2nd-century **villa** (www.coopculture.it) is one of Rome's least-visited major sights. It was the lavish home of two consuls, the Quintili brothers, but its luxurious excess was their downfall: the emperor Commodus had them both killed and seized the villa for himself. The emperor expanded the complex and the remaining ruins retain their opulence. Don't miss the baths complex with a pool, *caldarium* (hot bath room) and *frigidarium* (cold bath room) and the small museum, which offers useful context.

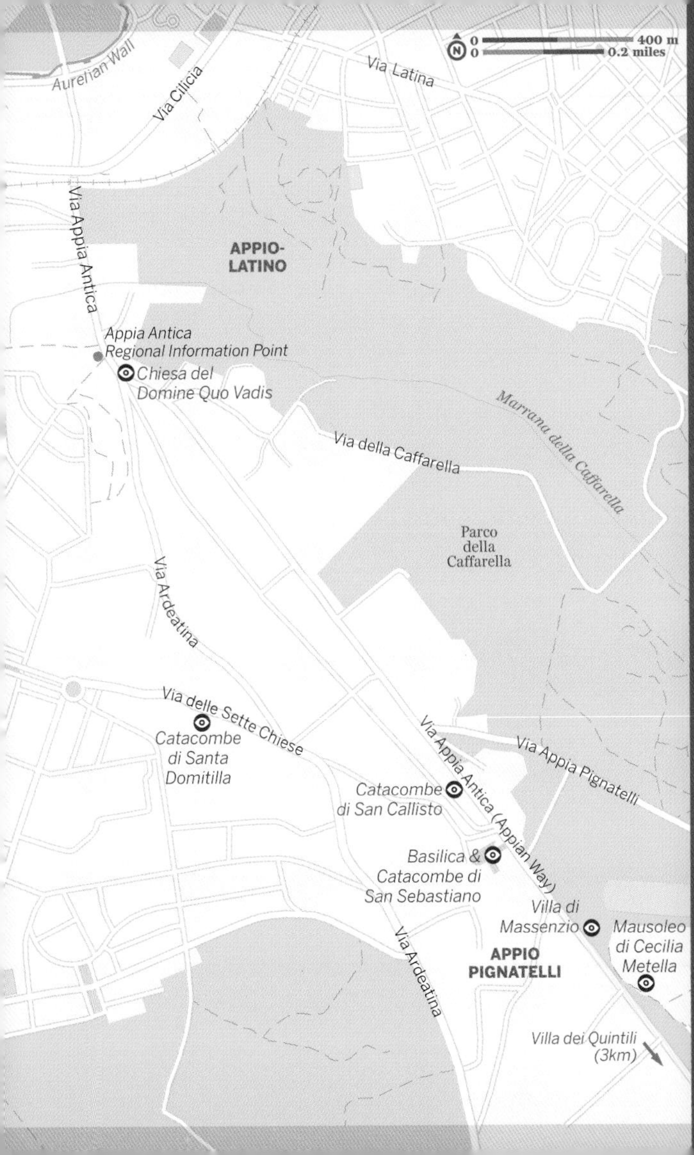

N

0   400 m
0   0.2 miles

Via Latina

Aurelian Wall

Via Cilicia

Via Appia Antica

**APPIO-
LATINO**

Appia Antica
Regional Information Point
◉ Chiesa del
Domine Quo Vadis

Via della Caffarella

Marrana della Caffarella

Parco
della
Caffarella

Via Ardeatina

Via delle Sette Chiese

◉ Catacombe
di Santa
Domitilla

Via Appia Antica (Appian Way)

Via Appia Pignatelli

◉ Catacombe
di San Callisto

Basilica &
Catacombe di
San Sebastiano ◉

Villa di
Massenzio ◉

Mausoleo
di Cecilia
Metella
◉

**APPIO
PIGNATELLI**

Via Ardeatina

Villa dei Quintili
(3km) ↘

Explore

Trastevere & Gianicolo

Trastevere's otherness is clear from its name, which literally means 'across the Tiber'. This charismatic neighbourhood combines cobbled lanes, ivy-draped palazzi, and a fiercely local identity. Its labyrinthine backstreets heave after dark as crowds stream to its restaurants and bars. Rising behind it all, Gianicolo (Janiculum Hill) offers soul-lifting views across faded-peach domes and towers.

The Short List

○ **Basilica di Santa Maria in Trastevere (p160)** *Gazing at shimmering medieval mosaics in this beautiful church.*

○ **Trattoria dining (p167)** *Feasting on Roman food amid the hubbub at traditional trattorias.*

○ **Villa Farnesina (p165)** *Savouring Raphael's interior decor at this elegant Renaissance villa.*

○ **Gianicolo (p166)** *Meandering up to the top of Rome's highest hill for dreamlike panoramas.*

Getting There & Around

🚋 Trams 3 (via Villa Borghese, San Giovanni and Colosseo) and 8 (from Largo Argentina).

🚌 Bus H from Termini; bus 780 from Piazza Venezia. For Gianicolo, bus 870 from Piazza della Rovere, bus 115 from Viale di Trastevere.

Neighbourhood Map on p164

Trastevere POLUDZIBER/SHUTTERSTOCK ©

Top Experience 📷
Admire Basilica di Santa Maria in Trastevere

⊙ MAP P164, B3

Lined by columns from the Terme di Caracalla and gilded with medieval mosaics, this church is said to be the oldest church in Rome dedicated to the Virgin Mary. It was first constructed in the early 3rd century over the spot where, according to legend, a fountain of oil miraculously sprang from the ground. Its current Romanesque form is the result of a 12th-century revamp.

Facade

The church facade is decorated with a beautiful medieval mosaic depicting Mary feeding Jesus surrounded by 10 women bearing lamps. Two are veiled and hold extinguished lamps, symbolising widowhood, while the lit lamps of the others represent their virginity. The portico was added by Carlo Fontana in 1702, with its balustrade decorated with statues of four popes.

Mosaics

Inside, it's the golden 12th-century mosaics that stand out. In the apse, look out for the dazzling depiction of Christ and his mother flanked by various saints and, on the far left, Pope Innocent II holding a model of the church. Beneath this is a series of six mosaics by Pietro Cavallini (c 1291) illustrating the life of the Virgin.

Interior Design

Note the 24 Roman columns, some plundered from the Terme di Caracalla; the fragments of Roman carved marbles forming an informal mosaic on the porch; the wooden ceiling designed in 1617 by Domenichino; and, on the right of the altar, a spiralling Cosmati candlestick, on the exact spot where the oil fountain is said to have sprung. The Cappella Avila is also worth a look for its stunning 17th-century dome. The spiralling Cosmatesque floor was relaid in the 1870s, a re-creation of the 13th-century original.

★ Top Tips

o Allow plenty of time to linger on the piazza in front of the church afterwards – it's Trastevere's focal square and a prime people-watching spot.

o Visit early in the morning or at the end of the day when the softer light shows off the beautiful Romanesque facade fresh from a painstaking restoration.

✗ Take a Break

Grab a cappuccino or a glass of Rome's cheapest beer, rubbing shoulders with everyone from grungy nightowls to old ladies, at Bar San Calisto (p169), a local haunt just footsteps from the touristy church square.

Get a slice of some of Trastevere's best pizza at La Renella (p167), the available varieties change by the minute.

Walking Tour 🥾

A Night Out in Trastevere & Gianicolo

Everyone loves to amble around Trastevere's cobbled lanes on balmy evenings, and there's a carnival atmosphere nightly, with street sellers, pavement restaurants and bars, and plenty of people wandering some of Rome's prettiest streets. Foreigners love it, but it's also a local haunt, and Romans come here in droves.

Walk Facts

Start Piazzale Giuseppe Garibaldi; bus 115, 870

End Niji Roma; bus Belli

Length 1.8km; four hours

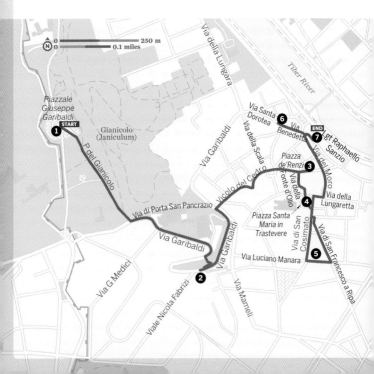

❶ Gianicolo Panoramas

Start your walk on a literal high. The early evening is a good time to enjoy sweeping, glorious views from the **Gianicolo** (p166). This leafy hill, Rome's highest, was the scene of vicious fighting during Italian unification but is now a tranquil, romantic spot, and one of the best viewpoints in Rome.

❷ Ombre Rosse

One of Trastevere's favourite bars, full of locals as well as tourists, **Ombre Rosse** (p169) is handily located en route from the Gianicolo. It's a chic place for a sundowner accompanied by a few delicious snacks, with the terrace offering some lovely views over Trastevere rooftops.

❸ Dinner at Da Augusto

Queue for a rickety table on an atmospheric Trastevere piazza at **Da Augusto**. Open since 1887, order from rushed-off-their-feet waiters and tuck into big plates of pasta at this family-run, no-fuss favourite. All the Roman classics are dished up here, with specials changing according to the season. Bathrooms are basic.

❹ People-watch on Piazza di Santa Maria in Trastevere

Trastevere's main square, **Piazza di Santa Maria in Trastevere**, is prime people-watching territory. By day it's full of cheery locals and guidebook-toting tourists; by night foreign students, marauding Romans and hijinks-minded visitors take over.

❺ Gelato at Otaleg

Spot **Otaleg** (p167) (gelato spelled backwards) by the queue. Gelato-master Marco Radicioni produces creamily delicious *zabaglione*, pistachio, and dark chocolate, using only the milk of grass-fed cows, or seasonal surprises like prickly pear and acacia honey.

❻ Beer at Ma Che Siete Venuti a Fà

Named after a football chant, which translates politely as 'What did you come here for?', this pint-sized Trastevere **pub** (p169) is a key address for Rome's craft beer scene, packing in around 15 international craft beers on tap and even more by the bottle.

❼ Drinks at Freni e Frizioni

Drop by to the enduringly popular Trastevere **Freni e Frizioni** (www. freniefrizioni.com), whose name means 'brakes and clutches' (this was once a mechanic's garage), and whose clientele spill out to sit on the wall of the small piazza.

CENTRO STORICO

0 ――――― 200 m
0 ――――― 0.1 miles

Lgt della Farnesina

Via della Lungara

Via Giulia

Via dei Monserrato

Via del Giubbonari

REGOLA

Lgt dei Tebaldi

Tiber River

SANT' ANGELO

Via Arenula

27 21

Via dei Riari

17 Villa
2 Farnesina

3 Galleria Corsini

6 Orto Botanico

2

Gianicolo
(Janiculum)

Ponte
Sisto

Via dei Pettinari

Via delle Zoccolette

Lgt dei Vallati

Lgt de Cenci

Via Benedetta

17 Piazza
Trilussa

14

Via del
Politeama

Ponte
Garibaldi

**Isola
Tiberina**

19

Vic del
Cinque

Via del Moro

Lgt Raphaello Sanzio

Ponte
Cestio

Via Garibaldi

Via del
Mattonato

Via della Scala

20

10

Via Renella

Piazza
Belli

Sora
Mirella
Caffè

Piazza
Sant'Egidio

Via della
Lungaretta

8

Piazza
Sonnino

Piazza in
Piscinula

3 Tempietto di
Bramante &
Chiesa di San Pietro
in Montorio

16

Basilica di
Santa Maria
in Trastevere

Via della Luce

25

Via dei Salumi

12

4

5

Gianicolo

Via Luciano Manara

9 Via di San Francesco a Ripa

TRASTEVERE

Via dei
Vascellari

11

18

Via Garibaldi

Via Mameli

13

Piazza San
Cosimato

24

15

Piazza
Mastai

Via della Luce

7

26

Via Morosini

Via di Trastevere

23

Basilica di 1
Santa Cecilia
in Trastevere

Via di Santa
Cecilia

22

Via Anicia

Viale di Trastevere

Via di San Michele

5

Via F Casini

Viale Glorioso

Piazza di
San Francesco
d'Assisi

Porta di Ripa Grande

Lgt Aventino

Piazza
dell'Emporio

Mercato di
Porta Portese

Piazza di
Porta
Portese

Ponte
Sublicio

6

Via Portuense

Tiber River

Via Marmorata

Lgt Testaccio

For reviews see	
◆ Top Experiences	p160
◉ Sights	p165
✕ Eating	p167
✦ Drinking	p169
✪ Entertainment	p170
🔒 Shopping	p170

Sights

Basilica di Santa Cecilia in Trastevere

BASILICA

1 MAP P108, D4

The last resting place of the patron saint of music is said to be built on the site of her house, and you can visit the Roman excavations below the church. Inside the church, Stefano Maderno's mysterious sculpture depicts St Cecilia's body apparently exactly as it was when it was unearthed in the Catacombs of San Callisto in 1599. You can also see Pietro Cavallini's exquisite 13th-century fresco in the nuns' choir of the hushed convent adjoining the church. (www.benedettinesantacecilia.it)

Villa Farnesina

HISTORIC BUILDING

2 MAP P108, A2

Commissioned by Sienese banker Agostino Chigi in the 16th century, this masterpiece of Renaissance architecture is a perfect marriage with its glorious interior frescoes. Prime among these are the ground-floor **Loggia of Cupid and Psyche** and the **Loggia of Galatea**, attributed to Raphael. On the 1st floor, Peruzzi's dazzling frescoes in the **Salone delle Prospettive** show an illusionary perspective of a colonnade and panorama of 16th-century Rome. (www.villafarnesina.it)

Trastevere & Gianicolo Sights

Villa Farnesina

ANNA PAKUTINA/SHUTTERSTOCK ©

Galleria Corsini

GALLERY

3 ◉ MAP P108, A2

Once home to the fascinating Queen Christina of Sweden, who abdicated and settled in Rome following her conversion to Catholicism, frequently dressed as a man, and entertained both male and female lovers here, this gallery is in a 16th-century palace designed by Ferdinando Fuga in grand Versailles style. It now houses some of Italy's national art collection, including Caravaggio's *San Giovanni Battista (St John the Baptist)* and Fra' Angelico's *Corsini Triptych*, plus works by Rubens, Poussin and Van Dyck. (www.barberinicorsini.org)

Tempietto di Bramante & Chiesa di San Pietro in Montorio

CHURCH

4 ◉ MAP P108, A3

Bramante's sublime *tempietto* (Little Temple; 1508) is a perfect surprise, a High Renaissance masterpiece, resonant with references to ancient Roman and Greek architecture, squeezed into the courtyard of the Chiesa di San Pietro in Montorio, on the spot where St Peter is said to have been crucified. It was commissioned by Philip and Isabella of Spain, as the church is dedicated to Rome's Spanish community. (www.sanpietroinmontorio.it)

Gianicolo

HILL

5 ◉ MAP P108, A4

It's worth the steepish walk up to the summit of Gianicolo (or Janiculum) hill for a stupendous view across Rome. The hill is dotted by monuments to Garibaldi and his makeshift army, who fought pope-backing French troops in one of the fiercest battles in the struggle for Italian unification on this spot in 1849. The Italian hero is commemorated with a massive **monument** in Piazzale Giuseppe Garibaldi, while his Brazilian-born wife, Anita, has her own **monument** about 200m away in Piazzale Anita Garibaldi; she died from malaria, together with their unborn child, shortly after the siege.

Orto Botanico

GARDENS

6 ◉ MAP P108, A2

Formerly the private grounds of Palazzo Corsini, Rome's 12-hectare botanical gardens are a little-known, forgotten-feeling gem and a great place to unwind in a tree-shaded expanse covering the steep slopes of the Gianicolo. Plants have been cultivated here since the 13th century and the current gardens were established in 1883, when the grounds of Palazzo Corsini were given to the University of Rome. They now contain up to 8000 species, including some of Europe's rarest plants.

Eating

Suppli
STREET FOOD €

7 ✖ MAP P108, B4

This blink-and-you-miss-it Trastevere *tavola calda* (hot table) has Roman street food down to an art. Locals queue for its namesake *suppli*: superb, hot-from-the-fryer risotto balls spiked with *ragù* (meat and tomato sauce) and mozzarella. The family-run eatery also gets top marks for pizza by the slice. Daily specials include gnocchi (Thursday) and fried fish and calamari (Tuesday and Friday). (www.suppliroma.it)

Fior di Luna
GELATO €

8 ✖ MAP P108, C3

Fior di Luna (Italian for 'moon blossom') is a contender for some of the best handmade gelato and sorbet in the city. The choice is limited but the taste is sensational: gelato is produced in small batches using natural, seasonal ingredients. (http://fiordiluna.com)

Otaleg
GELATO €

9 ✖ MAP P108, B4

Revered *gelataio* Marco Radicioni skilfully churns some of the capital's best gelato at this slick little store off Piazza San Cosimato. Otaleg (gelato spelled backwards) has a soft spot for the classics – think pistachio, lemon and dark chocolate – but proves delightfully experimental with seasonal combinations such as prickly pear and acacia honey. (www.otaleg.com)

Gianicolo Cannon

If you're meandering through Trastevere, or further afield, and hear a loud crack, panic not, it's just the midday cannon salute from the top of the Gianicolo. In 1847 Pope Pius IX ordered that a cannon fire blank shells at this time daily to set a standard for all the city's bells. Since 1904 it's been shot from the Gianicolo, as it's a little less disturbing from there, but it can still be heard across the city. It wasn't fired during the World Wars, but recommenced in 1959.

La Renella
BAKERY €

10 ✖ MAP P108, B3

Watch pizza masters at work at this historic, no-frills Trastevere bakery. Savour the wood-fired ovens, functional bar-stool seating and heavenly aromas of pizza, bread (get the *casareccia*, crusty Roman-style bread) and biscuits. Piled-high toppings (and fillings) vary seasonally, to the joy of everyone from punks with big dogs to old ladies with little dogs. It's been in the biz since 1870. (http://larenella.com)

Da Enzo
TRATTORIA €€

11 ✖ MAP P108, D4

Settle in for a voyage around the Roman classics at this tiny, staunchly traditional trattoria. Da Enzo carefully sources its produce,

Cool Down with Grattachecca

It's summertime, the living is easy, and Romans like nothing better in the sultry evening heat than to amble down to the river and partake of some *grattachecca* (crushed ice covered in fruit and syrup). It's the ideal way to cool down, and there are kiosks along the riverbank satisfying this very Roman need; try **Sora Mirella Caffè** (Map p108, D3), next to Ponte Cestio. Down by the water, shaved ice in hand, meander north along the river to **Ponte Sisto** and watch the madding crowds and marauding seagulls.

relying on farms in Lazio. The seasonal, deep-fried Jewish artichokes and the *pasta cacio e pepe* (cheese and black-pepper pasta) are highlights. Expect to wait a while for a table, even if you've booked. (www.daenzoal29.com)

Trattoria Da Teo
TRATTORIA €€

12 MAP P108, D4

One of Rome's classic trattorias, local favourite Da Teo proffers excellent Roman standards as well as seasonal specials built around products such as artichokes, zucchini flowers, *puntarelle* (a type of chicory), truffles, porcini mushrooms and *fragoline di bosco* (wild strawberries). In warm weather,

dine at one of the much-coveted outdoor tables on the backstreet piazza. Book ahead. (www.facebook.com/Trattoria.da.teo)

Zia Restaurant
FUSION €€€

13 MAP P108, A4

Having worked with chefs such as Gordon Ramsey and Georges Blanc, Antonio Ziantoni created Zia, set on the slopes of the Gianicolo, and already Michelin-starred. Feast on fanciful, creative dishes, such as lamb with honey and juniper or sea bass with cider and liquorice, in an elegant, Scandi-inspired interior. (www.ziarestaurant.com)

Trapizzino Trilussa
STREET FOOD €

14 MAP P108, B2

Stefano Callegari's popular Trapizzino franchise delivers a mash-up of a *tramezzino* sandwich and a slice of pizza. The resulting *trapizzino* is a pocket of crunchy pizza dough stuffed with fillings (often organic) of your choice, such as eggplant parmesan and meatballs. This branch offers sit-down tables and a well-stocked wine bar. (www.trapizzino.it)

Pizzeria Ai Marmi
PIZZA €

15 MAP P108, C4

Also called *l'obitorio* (the morgue) because of its vintage marble-slab tabletops, this is Trastevere's oldest and most popular pizzeria (it opened in 1931). Think super-thin bases, a clattering buzz, testy waiters, street tables and traditional fried starters (olives, courgette flowers, etc) to get you going. (http://facebook.com/aimarmi)

Drinking

Bar San Calisto

BAR

16 🚇 MAP P108, B3

Head to 'Sanca' for its basic, stuck-in-time atmosphere, cheap prices and large terrace that spills onto the square. Here you'll hang with everyone from old ladies to night-time sunglass wearers and curious tourists. Expect occasional late-night jam sessions.

Ma Che Siete Venuti a Fà

PUB

17 🚇 MAP P108, B2

Named after a football chant, which translates politely as 'What

did you come here for?', this pint-sized Trastevere pub is a beer-buff's paradise, packing in around 15 international craft beers on tap and even more by the bottle. (www.football-pub.com)

Ombre Rosse

BAR

18 🚇 MAP P108, A4

This seminal Trastevere hangout has shifted to a superb location-with-a-view, albeit a little on the periphery of the district on the way to the Gianicolo hill. It's a cool, dolce vita spot, full of Romans and a great place to grab a drink and a seat on the terrace. (www.ombrerosseintrastevere.it)

Pizzeria Ai Marmi

Enoteca l'Antidoto WINE BAR

19 MAP P108, B3

In a quieter Trastevere backstreet, this is an enoteca specialising in natural wines, frequented by those in the know. Wine here is by the bottle, not the glass. (www.enotecalantidoto.com)

Mescita Ferrara WINE BAR

20 MAP P108, B3

Close to the busy hub of Piazza Trilussa, this tiny, sophisticated bar inside the entrance to upmarket restaurant Enoteca Ferrara serves delectable *aperitivo* and has a wide range of wines by the glass – perfect for an intimate tête-à-tête while the hordes rollick outside in Trastevere's party central. (www.enotecaferrara.it)

Porta Portese Market

Head to the mammoth **Mercato di Porta Portese** (Map p108, C5) flea market to see Rome bargain-hunting. Thousands of stalls sell everything from rare books and fell-off-a-lorry bikes to Peruvian shawls and off-brand phones. It's crazily busy and a lot of fun. Keep your valuables safe and wear your haggling hat for the inevitable discovery of a treasure amid the dreck.

Caffè Lungara 1940 CAFE

21 MAP P108, A1

Run with much pride, passion and creativity by the Nardecchia family for almost 80 years, Caffè Lungara is an address Romans, from students to arts-loving elderly couples, love. Pop in before or after visiting the neighbouring botanical gardens, Galleria Corsini or Villa Farnesina for a cappuccino, Aperol *spritz* sundowner or full meal in a sharp, bright, white interior. (http://lungara1940.com)

Entertainment

Lettere Caffè BAR

22 MAP P108, C5

Like books? Poetry? Blues, folk and jazz? Then you'll love this place: a clutter of bar stools and books, where there are regular live gigs, poetry slams, book launches and DJ sets. (www.facebook.com/lettere.caffe)

Big Mama BLUES

23 MAP P108, C5

Wallow in the Italian blues at Big Mama, a Trastevere basement. There are often several bands a night playing, with lots of atmosphere, cramped tables and virtuoso musicians. (www.bigmama.it)

Shopping

Antica Caciara Trasteverina
FOOD & DRINKS

24 MAP P108, B4

Open since 1900, this is a historic cheese shop, where the sought-after fresh ricotta is usually gone by lunchtime. If you're too late, take solace in the luscious *ricotta infornata* (oven-baked ricotta), wheels of *pecorino romano,* Sicilian anchovies, gourmet pasta and local wines. The lovely staff are knowledgable and friendly, and will plastic-wrap cheese and hams for transport home. (www.facebook.com/anticacaciaratrasteverina)

Biscottificio Innocenti   FOOD

25 MAP P108, D4

For homemade biscuits, bite-sized meringues and fruit tarts large and small, there is no finer address in Rome than this vintage *biscottificio* with ceramic-tiled interior, fly-net door curtain and a set of old-fashioned scales on the counter to weigh biscuits (€17 to €25 per kilo). The shop has been run with much love and passion for several decades by the ever-dedicated Stefania. (www.facebook.com/biscottificioInnocenti)

Les Vignerons   WINE

26 MAP P108, A4

If you're looking for interesting vintages, search out this lovely wine shop near the Mercato di Piazza San Cosimato. It has an excellent collection of natural wines, mainly from small Italian and French producers, as well as a comprehensive selection of spirits and international craft beers. Friendly

staff can help inform your choices. (www.lesvignerons.it)

Spazio Giallo   DESIGN

27 MAP P108, A1

To see some cutting-edge local design and homeware, head to this delightful shop-gallery, where homewares and art, curated by Carolina Levi and Cristiana Pacifico, are set against the brilliant yellow (giallo) walls.

Survival Guide

Trastevere (p159) RESUL MUSLU/SHUTTERSTOCK ©

Before You Go

Book Your Stay

○ Rome is expensive and busy; book ahead to secure the best deal.

○ Accommodation ranges from palatial five-star hotels to hostels, B&Bs, *pensioni* and private rooms; there's also a growing number of boutique suite and apartment hotels.

○ Everyone overnighting in Rome pays the *tassa di soggiorno*, a room-occupancy tax on top of their bill: €3 per person per night in one- and two-star hotels; €3.50 in B&Bs and room rentals; €4/6/7 in three-/four-/five-star hotels.

○ When you check in, you'll need to present your passport or ID card.

Useful Websites

○ **Lonely Planet** (www.lonelyplanet.com/italy/rome/hotels) Author-reviewed accommodation options.

○ **Cross Pollinate** (www.cross-pollinate.com)

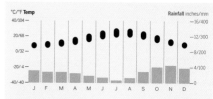

When to Go

○ **Winter (Dec–Feb)** Cold, short days. Museums are quiet and prices are low, except at Christmas and New Year.

○ **Spring (Mar–May)** Warm, sunny weather. Fervent Easter celebrations and azaleas on the Spanish Steps. Busy, with high prices.

○ **Summer (Jun–Aug)** Very hot. Plenty of outdoor events. In August, Romans desert the city and hoteliers drop prices.

○ **Autumn (Sep–Nov)** Popular period. Warm weather, high prices and the Romaeuropa festival. November brings rain and low-season prices.

Personally vetted rooms and apartments by the team behind Rome's **Beehive** (www.the-beehive.com) hostel.

○ **Bed & Breakfast Italia** (www.bbitalia.it) Italian B&B network listing many Rome options.

○ **ROMAC** (https://stayromac.com) Apartment and vacation-home rentals.

○ **Rome As You Feel** (www.romeasyoufeel.com) Apartment rentals: studio flats to luxury apartments.

○ **Italy Perfect** (www.italyperfect.com) Plenty of Rome apartment rentals.

○ **Ecobnb** (www.ecobnb.it) Booking site that rates eco-friendly places.

Best Budget

○ **RomeHello** (https://theromehello.com) Fabulous street art–adorned hostel operated as a social enterprise.

○ **Althea Inn Roof Terrace** (www.altheainnroofterrace.com) Designer comfort at budget prices.

○ **Beehive** (www.the-beehive.com) Sustainable, friendly and stylish hostel near Termini.

○ **Yellow** (www.the-yellow.com) A 374-bed party hostel with epic add-ons and facilities.

○ **Hotel San Pietrino** (www.sanpietrino.it) Family-run *pensione* within easy walking distance of the Vatican.

Best Midrange

○ **Residenza Maritti** (www.residenzamaritti.com) Hidden treasure with captivating views over the forums.

○ **Mama Shelter Rome** (https://mamashelter.com/roma) A fun, hip hotel with fabulous facilities.

○ **Arco del Lauro** (www.arcodellauro.it) B&B bolthole with ultra-friendly hosts.

○ **66 Imperial Inn** (www.66imperialinn.com) Bright and comfortable rooms with plenty of extras.

○ **Relais Le Clarisse** (www.leclarissetrastevere.com) Rooms around a tranquil courtyard in bustling Trastevere.

○ **Casa Fabbrini: Campo Marzio** (https://campomarzio.casafabbrini.

it) Style on a budget in upmarket Tridente.

Best Top End

○ **Soho House Rome** Laid-back, mid-century glamour and a rooftop pool.

○ **Chapter Roma** (www.chapter-roma.com) A cool urban bolthole on the edge of the Ghetto.

○ **Eitch Borromini** (www.eitchborromini.com) Elegant rooms and two roof terraces overlooking Piazza Navona.

○ **Palazzo delle Pietra** (www.palazzodellepietre.com) Glamorous Roman style in a historic *palazzo*.

○ **Palazzo Scanderbeg** (www.palazzoscanderbeg.com) Sleek contemporary suites in a 15th-century *palazzo*.

Arriving in Rome

Leonardo da Vinci Airport (Fiumicino)

Rome's main international airport, **Leonardo da Vinci**

(www.adr.it/fiumicino), aka Fiumicino, is 30km west of the city. It currently has two operational terminals, T1 and T3, both within walking distance of each other.

The easiest way to get into town is by train, but there are also buses and private shuttle services.

Leonardo Express (www.trenitalia.com) Runs to/from Stazione Termini. Departures from the airport every 30 minutes. Journey time is approximately 30 minutes.

FL1 (www.trenitalia.com) Connects to Trastevere, Ostiense and Tiburtina stations, but not Termini. Departs every 15 minutes (half-hourly on Sundays and public holidays).

SIT Bus (www.sitbusshuttle.com) Regular departures to **Via Marsala** outside Stazione Termini. All buses stop near the Vatican (Via Crescenzio 2) en route. Tickets are available on the bus. Journey time is approximately one hour.

Cotral (www.cotralspa.it) Runs between Fiumicino and Stazione Tiburtina via Termini. Four to six daily departures including night services from the airport and Tiburtina. Journey time is one hour.

Schiaffini Rome Airport Bus (www.romeairportbus.com) Regular services between the airport and Stazione Termini (Via Giolitti). Allow about an hour for the journey.

TAM (www.tambus.it) Runs buses from/to the airport to Via Giolitti 34 outside Stazione Termini at least hourly all night. Reckon on 40 minutes to one hour journey time.

Airport Connection Services (www.airportconnection.it) Transfers to/from the city centre start at €22 per person (€28 for two).

Airport Shuttle (www.airportshuttle.it) Transfers to/from your hotel for €44 for up to two people, then €6 for each additional passenger up to a maximum of eight.

Taxi The set fare to/from the city centre is €50, which is valid for up to four passengers including luggage. Note

that taxis registered in Fiumicino charge more, so make sure you catch a Comune di Roma taxi – these are white with a taxi sign on the roof and Roma Capitale written on the door along with the taxi's licence number. Journey time is approximately 45 to 60 minutes depending on traffic.

Ciampino Airport

Ciampino (www.adr.it/ciampino), 15km southeast of the city centre, is used by Ryanair (www.ryanair.com) for European and Italian destinations. It's not a big airport, but there's a steady flow of traffic, and at peak times it gets extremely busy.

To get into town, the best option is to take one of the dedicated bus services. Alternatively, you can take a bus to Ciampino station and then pick up a train to Termini or get a bus to Anagnina metro station (on line A).

SIT Bus (www.sitbusshuttle.com) Regular departures between the airport and **Via Marsala** outside

Stazione Termini. Get tickets online, on the bus or at the desk at Ciampino. Journey time is 45 minutes.

Terravision (www.terravision.eu) Runs between the airport and Stazione Termini. Bank on 45 minutes for the journey.

Atral (www.atral-lazio.com) Runs regular buses between the airport and Anagnina metro station (€1.20) and Ciampino train station (€1.20), from which you can get a train to Termini (€1.50).

Airport Connection Services (www.airportconnection.it) Transfers to/from the city centre start at €22 per person (€28 for two).

Airport Shuttle (www.airportshuttle.it) Transfers to/from your hotel for €25 for one person, then €6 for each additional passenger up to a maximum of eight.

Taxi The set rate to/from the airport is €31. Journey time is approximately 30 minutes, depending on traffic.

Stazione Termini & Bus Station

o Rome's main station and principal transport hub is **Stazione Termini** (www.romatermini.com). It has regular connections to other European countries, all major Italian cities and many smaller towns. High-speed regional services are run by Le Frecce or Italo. Book ahead for the best prices.

o Train information is available from the Customer Service area on the main concourse to the left of the ticket desks. Alternatively, check www.trenitalia. com or phone 89 20 21.

o From Termini, you can connect with the metro or take a bus from Piazza dei Cinquecento out front. Taxis are outside the main entrance/ exit.

o **Left Luggage** is available by platform 24 on the Via Giolitti side of the station.

Getting Around

Metro

o Rome has two main metro lines, A (orange) and B (blue), which cross at Termini. A branch line, B1, serves the northern suburbs, while work continues on a third line, C, which currently runs through the southeastern outskirts from San Giovanni. However, you're unlikely to need these two lines.

o Trains run between 5.30am and 11.30pm (to 1.30am on Fridays and Saturdays).

o Take line A for the Trevi Fountain (Barberini), Spanish Steps (Spagna) and St Peter's (Ottaviano–San Pietro).

o Take line B for the Colosseum (Colosseo).

Bus

o Rome's public bus service is run by **ATAC** (www.atac.roma.it).

o The **main bus station** is in front of Stazione Termini on Piazza dei Cinquecento, where there's an **information booth**.

o Other important hubs are at Largo di Torre Argentina and Piazza Venezia.

o Buses run 24 hours, although at night they are less frequent.

o Rome's night bus service comprises more than 25 lines, many of which pass Termini and/or Piazza Venezia. Buses are marked with an 'n' before the number and bus stops have a blue owl symbol. Departures are usually every 15 to 30 minutes, but can be much slower.

For route planning and real time information, Roma Bus is a useful phone app.

Cycling & Electric Scooters

Electric scooters are everywhere and are a popular way for tourists to get around given the scale of the city. Rent them via apps like Bird, Dott, Lime, Helbiz or Wind. Prices start at €0.15 per minute.

Tickets & Passes

Public transport includes buses, trams, metro and a suburban train network. The main hub is Stazione Termini. Tickets are valid on all buses, trams and metro lines, except for routes to Fiumicino airport. Ticket options include:

BIT (a single ticket valid for 100 minutes; in that time it can be used on all forms of transport but only once on the metro) €1.50

Roma 24h (24 hours) €7

Roma 48h (48 hours) €12.50

Roma 72h (72 hours) €18

CIS (weekly ticket) €24

Abbonamento mensile (a monthly pass) For a single user €35

Children under 10 travel free.

Buy tickets from *tabacchi* (tobacconist's shops), newsstands and vending machines at main bus stops and metro stations. Validate in machines on buses, at metro entrance gates or at train stations. Ticketless riders risk a fine of €54.90.

You can also buy and validate tickets through the MyCicero app once it's connected to your payment card.

The Roma Pass (48/72 hours €32/52) comes with a travel pass valid within the city boundaries.

Likewise, cycling is increasingly popular given the expanding network of dedicated cycle paths. Pick up electric bikes via apps like Lime and Helbiz. Take note though, bikes are less maneuverable in the tiny lanes of the *centro storico*.

Tram

Rome has a limited tram network. For route maps see www.atac.roma.it.

The most useful services:

○ **Line 2** Piazzale Flaminio to/from Piazza Mancini.

○ **Line 3** Museo Nazionale Etrusco di Villa Giulia to/from San Lorenzo, San Giovanni, Testaccio and Trastevere.

○ **Line 8** Piazza Venezia to/from Trastevere.

○ **Line 19** Piazza del Risorgimento to/from Villa Borghese, San Lorenzo and Via Prenestina.

Taxi

○ Official licensed taxis are white with a taxi sign on the roof and Roma Capitale written on the front door along with the taxi's licence number.

○ Always go with the metered fare, never an arranged price (the set fares to/from the airports are exceptions).

○ Official rates are posted in taxis and at https://romamobilita.it/it/media/muoversiaroma/muoversi-taxi.

○ You can hail a taxi, but it's often easier to wait at a rank or phone for one. There are taxi

Buses from Termini

From Piazza dei Cinquecento, outside Stazione Termini, buses run to all corners of the city.

Destination	Bus No
St Peter's Sq	40/64
Piazza Venezia	40/64
Piazza Navona	40/64
Campo de' Fiori	40/64
Pantheon	40/64
Colosseum	75
Terme di Caracalla	714
Villa Borghese	910
Trastevere	H

ranks at the airports, Stazione Termini, Piazza della Repubblica, Piazza Barberini, Piazza di Spagna, Piazza Venezia, the Pantheon, the Colosseum, Largo di Torre Argentina, Piazza Belli, Piazza Pio XII, Piazza del Risorgimento.

○ To book, call the automated **taxi line** (in Italian 06 06 09) or use the ChiamaTaxi app.

○ MyTaxi is another good app. It allows you to order a taxi without having to deal with potentially tricky language problems.

Essential Information

Accessible Travel

○ Cobbled streets, paving stones, blocked pavements and tiny lifts are difficult for wheelchair users, while the relentless traffic can be disorienting for partially sighted travellers or those with hearing difficulties.

○ If you have an obvious disability and/or appropriate ID, many museums and galleries offer free admission for yourself and a companion.

○ To reach the city from Fiumicino, the wheelchair-accessible Leonardo Express train runs to Stazione Termini. Alternatively, **Fausta Trasporti** (http://accessibletransportation-rome.com) is one of a number of operators offering transfers in wheelchair-accessible vehicles.

○ If travelling by train, ring 800 90 60 90 to arrange assistance. At Stazione Termini, the **Sala Blu Assistenza Disabili** (www.rfi.it/it) next to platform 1 can provide information on wheelchair-accessible trains and help with transport in the station. Contact the office 24 hours ahead if you know you're going to need assistance. There are similar offices at Tiburtina and Ostiense stations.

○ **Roman Roads Tours** (https://romanroadstours.com; Via dei Coronari 149) is a leading provider of golf cart tours. It offers excellent guided tours in electric carts that seat up to six people.

Tours range from one-to three-hour itineraries to tasting tours and tours by night, and can accommodate wheelchair users. Even pets are welcome!

○ All stations on metro line B have wheelchair access and lifts, except Circo Massimo, Colosseo and Cavour. On line A, Cipro and Termini are equipped with lifts.

○ Bus 590 covers the same route as metro line A. Buses and trams with the International Symbol of Access have ramps. Routes with disabled access are indicated on bus stops.

○ Some taxis are equipped to carry passengers in wheelchairs; ask for a taxi for a *sedia a rotelle* (wheelchair). **Fausta Trasporti** (http://accessibletransportationrome.com) and **3750** (www.3570.it) have wheelchair-accessible vehicles.

○ Download Lonely Planet's free Accessible Travel guides from https://shop.lonelyplanet.com/categories/accessible-travel.com.

Electricity

Type L
220V/50Hz

Type F
230V/50Hz

Business Hours

Banks 8.30am–1.30pm and 2.45pm–4.30pm Monday to Friday

Bars & cafes 7.30am–8pm, sometimes until 1am or 2am

Clubs 10pm–4am or 5am

Restaurants noon–3pm and 7.30pm–11pm (later in summer)

Shops 10am–7.30pm or 8pm Monday to Saturday, some also 11am–7pm Sunday; smaller shops 10am–1.30pm and 3.30pm–7.30pm Monday to Saturday; some shops are closed Monday morning

Money
ATMs

○ ATMs (known in Italy as *bancomat*) are widely available in Rome, and most will accept cards tied into the Visa, MasterCard, Cirrus and Maestro systems.

○ Most ATMs have a daily withdrawal limit of €250.

○ Always let your bank know when you're going abroad to prevent your

Discount Cards

Omnia Card (adult/reduced €129/59; valid for 72 hours) Includes fast-track entry to the Vatican Museums and admission to St Peter's Basilica, Basilica di San Giovanni in Laterano, & Carcere Mamertino. Free travel on hop-on hop-off Open Bus Vatican & Rome, plus unlimited public transport within Rome. Free entry to two sites, then 50% discount to extra sites. A 24-hour version is also available (€69). Details at www.omniakit.org.

Roma Pass (€52; valid for 72 hours) Includes free admission to two museums or sites, as well as reduced entry to extra sites, unlimited city transport and discounted entry to other exhibitions and events. The 48-hour Roma Pass (€32) is a more limited version. Details at www.romapass.it.

card being frozen when payments from unusual locations appear.

Credit Cards

○ All businesses in Italy are required to have the facility to accept card payments. However, some cheaper *pensioni* (pensions), trattorias, pizzerias and small shops may ask for cash. Don't rely on credit cards at smaller museums or galleries.

○ Major cards such as Visa, MasterCard, Eurocard, Cirrus and Eurocheques are widely accepted. Amex is also recognised, although it's less common than Visa or MasterCard.

Tipping

Romans are not big tippers, but the following is a rough guide:

○ **Taxis** Optional, but most people round up to the nearest euro.

○ **Restaurants** Service (*servizio*) is generally included; if it's not, a euro or two is fine in pizzerias and trattorias, no more than five to 10% in smart restaurants.

○ **Bars** Not necessary, although many people leave small change if drinking at the bar.

○ **Hotels** Tip porters about €5 at A-list hotels.

Public Holidays

Most Romans take their annual holiday in August. This means that many businesses and shops close for at least part of the month, particularly around Ferragosto (Feast of the Assumption) on 15 August.

Public holidays include:

Capodanno (New Year's Day) 1 January

Epifania (Epiphany) 6 January

Pasquetta (Easter Monday) March/April

Giorno della Liberazione (Liberation Day) 25 April

Festa del Lavoro (Labour Day) 1 May

Festa della Repubblica (Republic Day) 2 June

Festa dei Santi Pietro e Paolo (Feast of Sts Peter & Paul) 29 June

Dos & Don'ts

Do...

∘ Greet people in bars, shops, trattorias etc with a *buongiorno* (good morning) or *buona-sera* (good evening).

∘ Dress the part – cover up when visiting churches and go smart when eating out.

∘ Eat pasta with a fork, not a spoon; it's OK to eat pizza with your hands.

Don't...

∘ Feel you have to order everything on the menu. No one seriously expects you to eat a starter, pasta, second course and dessert.

∘ Order cappuccino after lunch or dinner. Well OK, you can, but Romans don't.

∘ Wait for cars to stop at pedestrian crossings. You'll have to make the first move if you want to cross the road.

Ferragosto (Feast of the Assumption) 15 August

Festa di Ognisanti (All Saints' Day) 1 November

Festa dell'Immacolata Concezione (Feast of the Immaculate Conception) 8 December

Natale (Christmas Day) 25 December

Festa di Santo Stefano (Boxing Day) 26 December

Safe Travel

Rome is a safe city, but petty theft can be a problem. Use common sense and watch your valuables.

∘ Pickpockets and thieves are active in touristy areas such as the Colosseum, Piazza di Spagna, Piazza Venezia and St Peter's Square.

∘ Be alert around Stazione Termini and on crowded public trans-port – the 64 Vatican bus is notorious.

∘ Avoid buying tickets for major sites, such as the Colosseum, from ticket touts.

∘ In case of theft or loss, always report the incident to the police within 24 hours and ask for a statement.

Telephone Services

∘ Local SIM cards can be used in European, Australian and unlocked US phones. Other phones must be set to roaming.

∘ Italian mobile phones operate on the GSM 900/1800 network, which is compatible with the rest of Europe and Australia but not always with the North American GSM or CDMA systems – check with your service provider.

∘ The cheapest way of using your mobile is to buy a prepaid *(prepa-gato)* Italian SIM card. TIM (Telecom Italia Mobile; www.tim.it), Wind (www.wind.it), Vodafone (www.vodafone.it) and Tre (www.tre.it) all offer SIM cards and have retail outlets across town.

o Note that by Italian law all SIM cards must be registered in Italy, so make sure you have a passport or ID card with you when you buy one.

Toilets

Public toilets are not widespread, but you'll find them at St Peter's Square (free) and Stazione Termini (€1). If you're caught short, the best thing to do is to nip into a cafe or bar.

Tourist Information

There are tourist information points at **Fiumicino** and **Ciampino** airports, as well as locations across the city:

o **Stazione Termini**
(www.turismoroma.it) In

the hall adjacent to platform 24.

o **Imperial Forums** (Map p50)

o **Via Marco Minghetti** Between Via del Corso and the Trevi Fountain.

o **Castel Sant'Angelo** (www.turismoroma.it)

For information about the Vatican, contact the **Ufficio Pellegrini e Turisti** (www.vatican.va).

Rome's official tourist website, **Turismo Roma** (www.turismoroma. it), has comprehensive information about sights, accommodation and city transport, as well as itineraries and up-to-date listings.

The **Comune di Roma** (www.060608.it) runs a free multilingual tourist information phone line providing info on culture, shows, hotels, transport etc. Its

website is also an excellent resource.

Visas

o Italy is one of the 26 European countries making up the Schengen area. The visa rules that apply to Italy apply to all Schengen countries.

o EU citizens do not need a visa to enter Italy – a valid ID card or passport is sufficient.

o Nationals of some other countries, including Australia, Canada, Israel, Japan, New Zealand, Switzerland, the UK and the USA, do not need a visa for stays of up to 90 days.

o Nationals of other countries will need a Schengen tourist visa – to check requirements see www. schengenvisainfo.com/ tourist-schengen-visa.

Language

Regional dialects are an important part of identity in many parts of Italy, but you'll have no trouble being understood in Rome or anywhere else in the country if you stick to standard Italian, which is what we've also used in this chapter.

The sounds used in Italian can all be found in English. If you read our pronunciation guides as if they were English, you'll be understood. The stressed syllables are indicated with italics. Note that *ai* is pronounced as in 'aisle', *ay* as in 'say', *ow* as in 'how', *dz* as the 'ds' in 'lids', and that *r* is a strong and rolled sound.

To enhance your trip with a phrasebook, visit lonelyplanet.com.

Basics

Hello.
Buongiorno.   bwon·*jor*·no

Goodbye.
Arrivederci.   a·ree·ve·*der*·chee

How are you?
Come sta?   *ko*·me sta

Fine. And you?
Bene. E Lei?   *be*·ne e lay

Please.
Per favore.   per fa·*vo*·re

Thank you.
Grazie.   *gra*·tsye

Excuse me.
Mi scusi.   mee *skoo*·zee

Sorry.
Mi dispiace.   mee dees·*pya*·che

Yes./No.
Sì./No.   see/no

I don't understand.
Non capisco.   non ka·*pee*·sko

Do you speak English?
Parla inglese?   *par*·la een·*gle*·ze

Eating & Drinking

I'd like ...   *Vorrei ...*   vo·*ray* ..

  a coffee   *un caffè*   oon ka·*fe*

  a table   *un tavolo*   oon *ta*·vo·lo

  the menu   *il menù*   eel me·*noo*

  two beers   *due birre*   doo·e *bee*·re

What would you recommend?
Cosa mi   *ko*·za mee
consiglia?   kon·*see*·lya

Enjoy the meal!
Buon appetito!   bwon a·pe·*tee*·to

That was delicious!
Era squisito!   e·ra skwee·*zee*·to

Cheers!
Salute!   sa·*loo*·te

Please bring the bill.
Mi porta il   mee *por*·ta eel
conto, per favore?   kon to per fa·*vo*·re

Shopping

I'd like to buy ...
Vorrei comprare ...   vo·*ray* kom·*pra*·re

I'm just looking.
Sto solo   sto *so*·lo
guardando.   gwar·*dan*·do

How much is this?

Quanto costa
questo?

kwan·to kos·ta
kwe·sto

It's too expensive.

È troppo caro/
cara. (m/f)

e tro·po ka·ro/
ka·ra

Emergencies

Help!
Aiuto! — a·yoo·to

Call the police!
Chiami la
polizia! — kya·mee la
po·lee·tsee·a

Call a doctor!
Chiami un
medico! — kya·mee oon
me·dee·ko

I'm sick.
Mi sento male. — mee sen·to ma·le

I'm lost.
Mi sono perso/
persa. (m/f) — mee so·no per·so/
per·sa

Where are the toilets?
Dove sono i
gabinetti? — do·ve so·no ee
ga·bee·ne·tee

Time & Numbers

What time is it?
Che ora è? — ke o·ra e

It's (two) o'clock.
Sono le (due). — so·no le (doo·e)

morning	mattina	ma·tee·na
afternoon	pomeriggio	po·me·ree·jo
evening	sera	se·ra
yesterday	ieri	ye·ree
today	oggi	o·jee

tomorrow	domani	do·ma·nee
1	uno	oo·no
2	due	doo·e
3	tre	tre
4	quattro	kwa·tro
5	cinque	cheen·kwe
6	sei	say
7	sette	se·te
8	otto	o·to
9	nove	no·ve
10	dieci	dye·chee
100	cento	chen·to
1000	mille	mee·le

Transport & Directions

Where's ...?
Dov'è ...? — do·ve ...

What's the address?
Qual'è
l'indirizzo? — kwa·le
leen·dee·ree·tso

Can you show me (on the map)?
Può mostrarmi
(sulla pianta)? — pwo mos·trar·mee
(soo·la pyan·ta)

At what time does the ... leave?
A che ora
parte ...? — a ke o·ra
par·te

Does it stop at ...?
Si ferma a ...? — see fer·ma a ...

How do I get there?
Come ci si
arriva? — ko·me chee see
a·ree·va

bus	l'autobus	low·to·boos
ticket	un biglietto	oon bee·lye·to
timetable	orario	o·ra·ryo
train	il treno	eel tre·no

Behind the Scenes

Send Us Your Feedback

We love to hear from travellers – your comments help make our books better. We read every word, and we guarantee that your feedback goes straight to the authors. Visit **lonelyplanet.com/contact** to submit your updates and suggestions.

Note: We may edit, reproduce and incorporate your comments in Lonely Planet products such as guidebooks, websites and digital products, so let us know if you are happy to have your name acknowledged. For a copy of our privacy policy visit lonelyplanet.com/legal.

Paula's Thanks

A great many thanks to Agnes Crawford for her insights, to Marco Angelini for his great tips and Giovanni Ursi for his music, thoughts and tips on this Eternal City. Thanks also to Laura and Lorenzo for sharing their apartment and recommendations, and to Angela Tinson at Lonely Planet for all her support along the way. Last, but not least, thanks to Rob for being the best partner in crime.

Acknowledgements

Cover photograph: Dome of St Peter's Basilica, Vatican; cge2010/ Shutterstock ©

Back photograph: Baths of Caracalla; Viacheslav Lopatin/Shutterstock ©

Photographs pp34-5 (clockwise from top left): Mazur Travel/ Shutterstock ©; Buffy1982/ Shutterstock ©; Takashi Images/ Shutterstock ©; Catarina Belova/ Shutterstock ©

This Book

This 8th edition of Lonely Planet's *Pocket Rome* guidebook was researched and written by Paula Hardy and Abigail Blasi. The previous edition was written by Duncan Garwood, Alexis Averbuck and Virginia Maxwell.

This guidebook was produced by the following:

Commissioning Editor Angela Tinson

Cartographer Wayne Murphy

Production Editor Margaret Milton

Book Designer Clara Monitto

Assisting Editor Carly Hall

Thanks to Ronan Abaywickrema, Darius Arya, Imogen Bannister, Agnes Crawford, Andrea Dobbin, Marco and Sererna Gigli, Carolina Levi, Johnny Ursi, Maja Vatrić

Index

See also separate subindexes for:

- **Eating p189**
- **Drinking p190**
- **Entertainment p190**
- **Shopping p191**

Our Writers

Paula Hardy

Paula has been a travel journalist for over 20 years. She was the commissioning editor of Lonely Planet's best-selling Italian list between 2005 and 2010, and has contributed to over 30 guidebooks covering the Italian peninsula from top to toe. She loves the energy of modern-medieval cities like Rome, and now divides her time between Milan, Venice and Marrakech. She is also a contributor to the *Financial Times*, *Telegraph* and the *Guardian*. You can follow her travels @paulahardy.

Abigail Blasi

Abigail has lived in Hong Kong, Rome, Copenhagen and London. She specialises in writing on Italy, Denmark, and India, but her travel writing has taken her from Tobago to Tunisia, and from Mauritania to Margate. As well as writing for Lonely Planet, she contributes to the *Telegraph*, *Times*, the *Independent*, *France Today*, and more.

Published by Lonely Planet Global Limited
CRN 554153
8th edition – April 2023
ISBN 978 1 83869 412 8
© Lonely Planet 2023   Photographs © as indicated 2023
10 9 8 7 6 5 4 3 2 1
Printed in Malaysia